HAYLEY HOBSON'S

Hip Guide to Creating Your

SEXY & ABUNDANT LIFE

WWW.HAYLEYHOBSON.COM

Cover and Book Design by Jane Ashley, **www.JaneScottBrandCatalysts.com**

DISCLAIMER OF HEALTH CARE RELATED SERVICES

All materials and content contained in this program are for general health information only and are not intended to be a substitute for professional medical advice, diagnosis or treatment.

Users of this program should not rely exclusively on information provided in this program for their own health needs. All specific medical questions should be presented to your own health care provider.

Hayley Hobson makes no warranties or representations, express or implied, as to the accuracy or completeness, timeliness or usefulness of any opinions, advice, services or other information contained or referenced in this program.

This information is based on my personal experience as a health coach.

Hayley Hobson, LLC encourages you to continue to visit and to be treated by your healthcare professionals; including, without limitation, a physician. Hayley Hobson is not acting in the capacity of a doctor, licensed dietician-nutritionist, psychologist or other licensed or registered professional. Hayley Hobson is not providing health care, medical or nutrition therapy services and will not diagnose, treat or cure in any manner whatsoever any disease, condition or other physical or mental ailment of the human body.

Upon purchasing this program, you understand that the information received should not be seen as medical or nursing advice and is certainly not meant to take the place of you seeing licensed health professionals.

~ Dedication ~

To my parents for their unwavering love.

To my husband, Wes, for his patience and understanding.

To my step-daughter, Makenna, for teaching me to soften.

And to my beloved daughter, Madeline, for allowing me to open my heart bigger than I ever thought I could.

Table of Contents

~ Acknowledgments ~

First I would like to thank my husband, Wes, who has supported my dreams and visions and given me the time to make this book a reality.

I would also like to thank my parents and my children for inspiring me every day.

I want to thank my teacher, Desiree Rumbaugh for helping me to see the light and beauty in every single moment.

And finally, I would like to thank my friend and assistant, Kelly Marceau for her focused determination, Scott Watrous and Jane Ashley-Watrous for believing in me and encouraging me to share my story, and Tami Wilson for her beautiful photography.

~ Introduction ~

If you're like me, you've got a lot going on. I hear it all the time—my family, friends and colleagues don't have any time. Not one extra minute. Our schedules are insane. We are probably the only culture in society that has taught ourselves how to talk, text, drive and eat all at the same time. Admit it. I'm not the only one, right?

You may be laughing but it's actually not funny.

Our world has become intense and we're falling deep into a massive hole we will not be able to climb out of if we don't start getting less busy.

But the problem is, none of our "obligations" are going away. We can't stop working. We're not going to stop raising families. And the expectations and pressures we put on ourselves—and that others put on us—keep growing. Boundaries have become blurred and answering the phone at 11pm or going out to dinner with friends, all on their iPhones, has become the norm.

It's no wonder that our country has the highest rate of cancer, Type 2 Diabetes, Heart Disease and Obesity than any other country. And don't forget depression, anxiety and prescription drug medication.

In this book I'm going to tell you stories that probably hit close to home. I'm going to make you laugh. I may make you cry. And if I do, you'll realize we are on the same path, living very similar dreams. And you know what? We are going to make it with these easy tips that will help you live a Sexy and Abundant Life.

In Chapter 1, I remind you how to connect with your inner vision and be so much more than perfect.

In Chapter 2, I give you easy steps you can follow to love what you're eating and feed your soul.

In Chapter 3, I motivate you to get your body moovin' and groovin'.

In Chapter 4, I remind you that you can have relationships that rock your world. And that means a relationship with your OWN body as well!

In Chapter 5, I teach you to nourish yourself and find time for YOU.

In Chapter 6, I show you how you can turn your passions into your career.

In Chapter 7, I help you find your inner goddess.

And in Chapter 8, I guide you towards finding the spirituality that lives deep within you.

By the time you get to the end of the book, you will have learned how to live with freedom, prosperity and compassion and turn it into a system that works for you.

MY STORY

TODAY IS THE ONE-YEAR ANNIVERSARY OF THE BEGINNING OF MY LIFE.

It's hard to believe it has been a year already. It's also hard to believe that I've come so far over the course of this past year. Really, it was just last Christmas Eve that I thought my life was ending. In fact, it was really just a beginning, and it led me to this seat to write my story.

Let me back up for a bit so you can get a clearer picture of where I was sitting before the main event.

Until last year, I thought I had it all figured out. My story is perhaps not unlike your own...I aimed for Wonder Woman status, and thought I could *DO* it all and *BE* it all.

Finally, having stopped listening to what my soul was telling me, everything inside me finally said "enough..."

Does this sound familiar to you?

Deep inhale. Most days, I woke up at 5:30 a.m. to run for an hour.

I quickly went into high gear, and within the next few hours, I had made the family breakfast, packed lunches, prepped dinner, and got the kids off to school. Then I practiced yoga and quickly took a shower to get ready for work. Being Wonder Woman, of course, meant I could never leave the house as is—looking like someone actually *lived* in it!—so before I headed out the door, the house was always magazine-shoot ready.

More deep inhaling. At work each day, I saw 3-4 private clients, taught 2-3 classes, and in-between, returned 100+ e-mails while managing a staff of 30 people.

Keep inhaling. When back at home after work, I cooked dinner, picked up the house (again), bathed the kids, and got back on my computer until 11 p.m. to catch up and prepare for the next day.

Has anyone said exhale yet?

Then I'd collapse. That is, until I had to start that exhausting routine all over, six hours later.

Looking back at how I lived this way, it gives me an anxiety attack just thinking about it. When did I fit in running errands, relaxing, socializing, or having fun?

You see, I thought I was doing everything right.

Cardio. *Check.*

Yoga. *Wouldn't miss it.*

Ambitious career. *Yes.*

There for the kids. *No doubt.*

Healthy diet. *Of course.*

Gluten-free. *A must.*

Clean house. *Always.*

Wasn't this the normal day of a "successful" woman in today's world?

So, whose idea was this woman's revolution thing anyway? When they said 'you can have it all,' did they realize how much **ALL** is? When did sleep become negotiable?

When did "doing nothing" become a sign of failure? When did relaxing and enjoying your husband, community, and friends become rewards instead of necessities? None of us even know what the word "connect" means anymore.

Wonder Woman's magic lasso forces those bound by it to tell the truth.

Well, one day last year, exactly one year ago, I found myself tied up in my own lasso and enslaved by my ambitions and perfectionism. I was finally forced to reassess my priorities, and re-evaluate my life.

My husband Wes and I packed up the car and got on the road embarking upon our 9 1/2 hour annual drive from Boulder to Kansas City to visit with my in-laws. Wes and I had had better times in our marriage in the past, to say the least, so the long drive seemed arduous to me before it even began.

How we had gotten to this point? Our life was glamorous on the outside, but it did not look pretty from the inside. We had a beautiful little two-year old girl and my husband had a gorgeous ten-year old daughter who lived with us half the time. We were in a brand new house we built at the foothills in Boulder, with a front lawn that encompassed acres of open space.

We both had jobs that should have allowed us the flexibility we wanted to create the schedule of our dreams—if we would have let ourselves. Yet something wasn't right. Our stress levels had risen to a point we couldn't manage and my body decided it had had enough.

We pulled into my in-laws driveway four days before Christmas like we always do. For those four days, the tension between my husband and I continued to exasperate me. *I was not smiling enough. I was working too much. I was not spending enough time with the family. I was not appreciative.* His complaints never stopped. By the time Christmas Eve arrived my gut was a wreck. I wished I could vanish. Disappear.

But of course, it was Christmas Eve! The family's biggest party of the year! Wes' sister, Lisa, was hosting 25 of us for dinner, as was the norm every year. Wes told me not to go but how could I not show up? What would that look like?

I arrived feeling miserable. Not only was I sad, lonely, depressed and exhausted, but I was nauseous as well. I felt like I was going to vomit. I wasn't sure how the hell I was going to get through this holiday extravaganza. Although barely speaking to Wes at this point, I confided in him that I felt sick to my stomach. My beloved, supportive husband's response?

"You just don't want to be here. Get your sh*t together."

I sat through the festive meal unable to put a morsel of food in my mouth, praying I wouldn't throw up all over the table. The night finally ended. I made it home and tried to fall asleep, meditating on the fact that I'd be feeling well by the morning. No luck. I lay there all night, knowing a bigger storm had entered my body. This storm was not going to pass overnight. But before I go further, I need to share a little bit about my relationship with my in-laws.

The relationship I have with my in-laws has always been challenging.

Even eight years later, I still question their feelings about me.

Wes was raised in a Christian home and I was raised in a Jewish one. From the time I started dating, my parents made it clear that they wanted me to marry a partner within the same faith. I did attempt to find one but I dated plenty of men that were not Jewish and I was never proud of the way my parents treated them. Don't misunderstand me. My parents are not prejudiced at all. They simply wanted the traditions I had learned to be carried down to the generations that came after them.

After agonizing years and disapproval from my own parents, I met Wes' parents and was even more shocked by their behavior. At this point I was 35 years old, divorced, and my parents had come to realize they would rather me be in a happy marriage than not married at all. I figured Wes' parents would feel the same way about their divorced son as well. Surprise! From the moment I met them, they made their feelings perfectly clear. They did not want Wes marrying anyone who was not a Christian. Over a decade battling with my own parents and now I was met with resistance of my soon to be husband's family. Great. I was never going to win this one.

I know Wes loved me, but he could not get rid of his parents' voices in his head. Although almost 40, he was unable to make a decision from deep within his own heart. Childhood insecurities lie deep, and his need to please did not end with adulthood. Wes' parents made the choice for me. He asked me to move out.

The reason I am sharing this short narrative is so you will realize how difficult it was for me to approach Wes' parents with the news that my marriage was deteriorating and I actually was in need of their help. Placing my pride aside, I began to communicate, share and beg that I be heard. The last thing I wanted was to end up divorced again.

I woke up on Christmas Day feeling even worse than the night before.

I stayed in my bed until 10am, wishing the nausea away. The entire family was downstairs waiting to celebrate what Santa had dropped off for the children the night before—but I couldn't stand up. Of course, Wes' response was less than sympathetic.

I couldn't get out of bed because the pain was so bad. I had started throwing up and I couldn't stop. I was stuck in Kansas City and the road home was a long one. I was miserable...

I don't know how we got there, but Boulder did eventually arrive much later that evening, after many pit-stops along the way. When you're feeling like I did, your first thought is a 24-hour stomach bug. Simple, right? Then 24 hours rolled into 48 hours and 48 hours rolled into 72 hours. The days rolled into a week. I was not getting any better. The pain and nausea were getting worse. It was hard to reach a doctor since the world was shutting down for the year. Eventually I ended up in the hospital. I was afraid...no one could figure out what was wrong.

Dehydration. Stomach Flu. Gas. Irritable Bowel. Inflammatory Bowel Disease. Stress. You name it, they mentioned it.

Over the next few weeks, I saw my family physician, who sent me back to the ER, who sent me to the radiology department, who sent me to see a surgeon, who sent me to the gastroenterologist. It was ridiculous. From one doctor's office to the next I went.

No one could figure out what was wrong. I was put on medication to stop the nausea. I was put on medication to stop the abdominal spasms. I was put on medication to help me sleep. I couldn't work. I was not eating. I could barely breathe. I could not hold my little girl.

My life had essentially stopped.

Growing up, traditional medical care was the norm.

My father was a radiologist. I had always instinctivly sought out that kind of help. Obviously, though, nothing prescribed was working. Did these guys really know how to diagnose? Were they simply ruling out what I did not have? Desperate, I decided I needed a more holistic approach, and I decided to explore chiropractic, aruyvedic care and life coaching.

I said, *"Up yours, diagnosis"* and got honest with myself.

What I've come to understand is that disease originates in four ways: congestion,

stagnation, depletion and deficiency. At that point, I was depleted. I was deficient. My body was in stagnation.

What was wrong with me, I came to realize, was that I hadn't allowed myself to stop moving. There was no time in my schedule for the slightest pause. My sympathetic nervous system had gone haywire, and my body was living in a constant state of fight or flight. The scariest part was that I didn't know differently. I was so used to it that I called it normal.

Thank God our bodies are designed to be smarter than our stubborn minds.

The next few months were a blur. I barely left the house. I had no choice but to cancel my chaotic schedule, that although the norm to me, would have given any of you an anxiety attack just looking at it in iCal.

This was the hardest part. I had been a work-a-holic. A perfectionist. The queen Bee of Type As. I had always rated my level of success based on how busy I could be. The more activities I had lined up on my plate, the more productive I felt. 10 minutes to spare? Perfect. Just enough time to run one more errand and then be stressed out in traffic.

preschool became an ordeal to me. Buying groceries and preparing a meal became an all day activity. When had there ever been time for everything else I had squeezed into my jam-packed schedule?

But shutting down for a while was exactly what my body, mind and soul needed in order to rejuvenate. It was time to go inward—to re-examine everything including my marriage, my relationships, my family, my business and career, money, my body, my fitness, my self-image, self-care, my spirituality and, of course, my health.

What did they mean to me? What did I want each area of my life to look like? What were my dreams? And why was I not there? What was stopping me? What was blocking me?

No more work. Some would consider that a gift. To me, it seemed like imprisonment.

No more exercise. Some would breathe a huge sigh of relief that someone or something had given them a hall pass. I felt lazy, stiff, fat and bored.

I slept in until after the sun came up.

I didn't get out of my pajamas oftentimes until mid-afternoon, if at all.

I couldn't imagine how I had been able to manage my life like it was until now. Just getting my daughter dressed and off to

It was time to take a very deep look. I did not want to be bound by the titles of mother, wife, daughter, manager, teacher, or athlete. I did not want to have to be perfect. All these expectations and roles were ones I had given myself in order to find a place in this world and have it all.

Once I slowed down, I was really able to connect with my true vision and become so much better than perfect. Now, perfection to me means less, not more. Slowing down. Not attacking the world from every angle. This way, less actually becomes more.

Once I slowed down, I was really able to connect with my true vision and become so much better than perfect.

Chapter 1
YOGA SEQUENCE

1. TADASANA
2. HALF SUN SALUTE
3. LOW LUNGE
4. LOW LUNGE W/TWISTS
5. CRESCENT LUNGE INTO GENTLE BACKBEND
6. GOAL POST ARMS
7. STANDING BACKBEND
8. UTTANASANA
9. STANDING SPLITS
10. VIRABHADRASANA 2
11. HUMBLE WARRIOR
12. CRESCENT LUNGE W/ARMS CLASPED BEHIND BACK
13. UTTANASANA
14. FOREARM PLANK
15. FOREARM DOG
16. PINCHAMYURASANA
17. VRKASANA W/BACKBEND
18. VINYASA
19. LOW LUNGE HOLDING BACK FOOT INTO BACKBEND
20. USTRASANA
21. URDHVA DANURASANA
22. PAVANMUKTASANA
23. JANU SIRSASANA
24. SAVASANA

HALF SUN SALUTE

SEE PAGE 12

PERFECTION-BACKBENDS

VINYASA
SEE PAGE 13

Visit **http://bit.ly/TxARZ5**
to access Hayley's downloadable
Yoga class, *Empowerment Flow*.

Additional
YOGA SEQUENCES

HALF SUN SALUTE

1. TADASANA
2. TADASANA WITH ARMS IN UTTITA HASTASANA
3. UTTANASANA
4. ARDHA UTTANASANA
5. UTTANASANA

SURYA NAMASKARA A/VINYASSA
(FULL SUN SALUTE)

1. TADASANA
2. TADASANA WITH ARMS IN UTTITA HASTASANA
3. ARDHA UTTANASANA
4. UTTANASANA
5. ADHO MUKHA SVANASANA
6. PLANK
7. CHATURANGA DANDASANA
8. UTTANASANA
9. ADHO MUKHA SVANASANA

~ Chapter 2 ~
FOOD

I WAS ALWAYS A SKINNY KID.

In fact, when I was 12, I was nicknamed "Kermie" because my legs were so scrawny, they resembled Kermit the Frog's legs. Not the most attractive name, but it stuck well into my college years. When skinny jeans became popular, I was discouraged because my butt was nonexistent and didn't blossom in my beautiful new pants like all the other girls in my class.

We've all had visions of our "ideal body" and my vision was simply to fill out my clothes! I spent years studying food and nutrition with the thought that if I put more nourishing foods into my body, I'd look even better. How vain I was!

Years later, I've learned it's not important what we look like on the outside but how we feel on the inside. I'm extremely particular about my diet because when I am, my body operates like a well-oiled machine. When I feel like I can conquer the world, the size of my jeans and the number on the scale become insignificant.

As I've matured, so has the size of my butt, but I feel better now in my 40s than I felt when I was 20. I'd like to share some of my thoughts with you about food.

My friends and family think I have an Eating Disorder.

About 25 years ago, I started suffering from World War III ransacking my gut. It was not only incredibly painful, but also extremely embarrassing. When I'd eat (or even mid-way through a meal,) I'd get horrendously bloated, have excruciating pain and have no idea what the culprit was.

Oftentimes, whatever bomb was exploding in my gut was so humiliating and painful I was afraid to do 'normal things' like go out to dinner with friends or head out to parties—and as a college student, I should have been attending. Instead, I'd stay home and lay in bed in fear of having to deal, yet again, with a massive explosion.

At the time, my diet consisted of the usual college staples: cereal, pizza, chips, donuts and alcohol. None of us had any money. The cafeteria scene sucked. None of us knew any better. We were living in an age of faster is best, so why not buy fast food?

There did come a point upon graduation when I just couldn't take it anymore. The doctors' visits had become endless and futile. The only information I continued to come home with was that I was lactose intolerant and I had an irritable bowel. So much for the pizza and fried food. I was going to have to come up with a better solution for my diet.

Even though I did cut dairy and fried food from my diet, my intestinal problems continued. I sought out homeopathic and aruyvedic doctors whose mission was to heal me from the inside out, eliminating all the foods that were causing inflammation in my bowel. I went back to school to receive a degree in **Integrative Nutrition** so that I could learn more about my condition and eventually have the knowledge to make choices that supported my health and well-being.

The elimination process continued. Alcohol, coffee and sugar were amongst the first to go. I also stopped eating gluten, beans, corn, any genetically modified soy product, most legumes, many nuts and most grains. The easiest diet for me to follow was a raw, vegan one with some warmer foods in the colder months.

Everyone around me, even my own family, thought I was obsessive. Obsessive because I had become health conscious? Obsessive because I was focusing on healthy foods that I had prepared myself? Foods that nourished and healed me from all of my suffering?

It's a tough call. I'm not sure I know the answer. I do refuse to eat in most restaurants, prepare 90% of my own food and carry what I need when I travel. I have to give myself an extra 15-minute leeway heading through security in the airport so all of my "pastes" can be tested for bombs. You'll never catch me in a Safeway, Ralph's or Publix, except to buy toilet paper and other household items. If I ever have to walk into a public "Supermarket" for food, I feel like I may have an anxiety attack! And of course, in most social situations I am made to feel like an outcast.

When I am invited out, friends and family go to the trouble of serving fruit and vegetables they claim are especially for me—and proudly show off the gluten-free alternatives they used. All I can think about is the factory-farmed meats that are still on their tables, the hormone-laden dairy they have absolutely no clue about, the possibility that all of the fruits and veggies are conventional and non-organic and the probability of sugar and genetically modified soy being added to everything. It can be a nightmare if I continue to obsess over it, but is it really taking over my life?

Right before Thanksgiving, I stumbled upon an article about a not-so-new, and not very well known eating disorder called Orthorexia. Steven Bratman, M.D. coined the term in a 1997 essay for *Yoga Journal* in which he described the disorder as a "fixation on eating proper food." Bratman, who himself had a food fixation while living on a commune in upstate New York, chose the prefix "ortho"—which in Greek means straight, correct, true—to reflect the obsession with maintaining a perfect diet.

When I first read about it, I almost couldn't believe it. Eating too healthy? That's a problem? Just who is classifying eating well as a disorder? The meat and dairy industry that is basically sleeping with our government? I was mortified. At first glance, though, it did seem as if the description completely reflected my stance on a perfect diet.

It continues to be my wish that more and more people will wake up and exercise a little more self control after they discover the toxicity of most of the foods in their diets, the consequences of not eating organic, and the hidden poisons disguised in ingredients they can't even pronounce. Becoming more health conscious is not just a growing fad for some people like me. It is a matter of do or die when we've been so afflicted with pain and even more serious issues or diseases like hyperthyroid, hypertension, high cholesterol, diabetes and even cancer.

Then I read further. Orthorexia, although not an official diagnosis, seems to include elements of other disorders such as anorexia and obsessive-compulsive disorder. So yes, it can be a serious problem and it may not help that people with orthorexia can receive positive feedback for behavior that may *appear* healthy. The key difference between orthorexia and simply following a strict diet is that orthorexia causes major distress to others and interferes with every day life. Orthorexics have sworn off most food groups, including all conventionally-grown food, and because of this, may even tend to grow a lot of their own food. Due to major eliminations in their diets, it is possible they could end up losing a lot of weight as well.

Today, after a complete overhaul in my diet, I feel alive and beaming with energy. I wake up when the sun comes up ready to go and maintain a steadiness all day long. I have to put myself to bed at night whereas before, I'd feel exhausted and exasperated by dinnertime. I'm eating foods that nourish me, give me strength and give me power. I feel like my digestive problems are completely under control. I'm not making choices out of self-deprivation or because I have a distorted, negative self-image. I'm making well-educated choices that have obviously healed my gut.

No one can tell you what you should or shouldn't eat. Only **YOU** can make that decision by pausing and becoming aware of the way that food affects your body, your moods, your attitude and your energy. Once you do, you will be able to reflect upon your choices and decide whether those choices serve you. I am proud of my choices and the only disorder I think I have is the disorder of even contemplating eating something that I know won't agree with me.

My husband would collect the evidence of countless cookie crumbs in our sheets before he climbed into bed next to me. I was caught red handed!

Flash back to earlier that night and you'd see me sitting in bed reading a Deepak Chopra book, (*Desperate Housewives* on in the background—cheesy tv shows are another bad habit of mine) with a stash of my addiction beside me. Crumbling chocolate chip cookies (yes, they were gluten-free) and a big bar of 73% dark chocolate.

Yep. you're hearing me correctly. The fitness and health-focused Hayley Hobson.

You don't believe me? I swear it's true. On nights when I'd turn in early, I used to eat my way through my stash before my husband would come to bed and find me innocently asleep, thinking I had gotten away with my sugar fix.

The next morning, inevitably, the guilt would be there as I awoke amongst a bed of crumbs; remorseful and grimacing as my husband poked fun of me.

Hi, my name is Hayley Hobson and I was once a sugar junkie.

The sugar fixes were giving me short, sweet (oh so sweet!) highs, but then they'd kick me into a slump a few hours later or worse, wake me up several times during the night. Then, to climb out of that slump, I'd eat more sugar and then, I'd put an IV drip of caffeine in my arm (not really, but I wished I could have!)

As you may be able to pick up so far, my methods were not working. I thought I could get away with my sugary habits since I was lean and athletic. What was really happening was that I was spiraling into an endless cycle that was wreaking havoc on my body, moods and energy. With my sweet tooth raging out of control, I decided it was time to lay down the needle (aka the boxes of cookies, coconut milk ice cream and choc-o-love bars) and pick up the greens. I committed to go cold turkey.

Can you relate? We have cravings because our diets are out of balance and then we eat sugar or processed foods in order to make us feel better. However, it's temporary and in the long run, debilitating. We go through an experience of feeling on top of the world and then we use caffeine to prevent ourselves from crashing into a slump when we feel it coming on.

We love the taste and feeling the sugar high gives us so much because of the chemical properties behind it. Sugar releases the feel-good chemical serotonin in our brain as well as endorphins that are in charge of making us happy and energized. It's a fix, and as any kind of junkie knows, fixes don't last long.

As a yoga and Pilates instructor, I need my body to be feeling flexible, supple and strong. With my obsession of eating Jelly Bellies, red licorice and Tootsie Rolls, I may have looked lean and mean, but that's not how I was feeling. I felt sluggish and blah— until I ate another Starburst to release more serotonin and help me feel nice.

I knew I needed to make a change, and that my commitment to nixing the sugar and eating more greens would benefit my career, family, and the people around me as well. My first step was to get OFF the caffeine. This was a hard one. When we're using caffeine, we can never really hear what our bodies are actually saying to us. We don't know we are tired because we're drugging ourselves to keep going faster and longer every day.

Next, I filled every plate with live food (lots of greens), complex carbohydrates, good fats and a complete protein. When our bodies are getting what we need in terms of nourishment, the cravings *do* go away. I promise.

Finally, I started to eat regularly again. Before, I would often skip breakfast or lunch because I was too busy (or jacked up on caffeine and not hungry) and then by mid-day I'd be dying for my sugar fixes or gluten-free pretzels. Many people skip meals for diet reasons or lifestyle reasons. It is one of the biggest counter-productive mistakes to make if you want to move toward a more energetic, healthy and fit lifestyle. By simply feeding your body regular meals, it loves you back by not craving the extra (and bad for you) food.

Greens are sugar's arch-enemy. I knew if I was going to put down that addiction with a Pilates body slam, greens were the way to go. I started by going to the farmer's market and picking out fresh, dark green veggies like spinach, kale and chard. Adding more of these into your diet is a great place to begin, as they are so rich in the nutrients our bodies crave.

Next, I realized dining out a lot was an obstacle to my goal, so I endeavored to make more healthy meals at home. This way I could understand what I was eating because I was buying it and cooking it myself. I felt better almost immediately with these small changes. By then I was inspired (and energized by my greens!) and I started juicing. I'd make a ton of green smoothies and eat a large array of vegetables ranging from fresh bok choy to mouth-watering avocados. Life was getting good, and not in a moment-by-moment way...that's saying a lot coming from an ex-sugar junkie!

The results I experienced became life changing for me and I began to study more and more about health and nutrition. My new lifestyle turned into my career. Now, the "icing on the cake" is living the life I love and feeling good, too!

Take it from an ex-junkie—you can get off the sugar and go green too!

My car just *accidentally* pulled into Burger King. What are YOU craving?

When I was 20 years old, I was diagnosed with IBS. That's what the doctors tell you when they can't figure out anything else wrong with you but you're obviously symptomatic. Over the next 10 years I was taken off gluten, dairy and other commonly known allergens such as soy, corn, peanuts legumes and beans, sugar, alcohol and fried food. Needless to say, I had a pretty clean diet.

Then I got pregnant. After 20 years of being dairy free and 10 years of being gluten free, I found my car *accidentally* pulling into Burger King one day and heard myself ordering a fried chicken sandwich. I have a photo of me eating it, which I will sell to the highest bidder.

For the next 3 months, all I wanted to eat were grilled cheese sandwiches, pancakes, french fries and barbecue-flavored potato chips. When I went in for my 20-week exam, my husband confided in our doctor that I had not eaten a vegetable or fruit in four months.

Our bodies are an incredible source of intelligence—they are always there for us, striving to maintain a perfect balance. So does this intelligence derail when you start to crave an entire box of chocolate or is it giving you critical information which will bring you back in balance?

We all have cravings. The questions become: a) why do we have them? and b) how can we deconstruct them? The answers help us understand what our bodies are really saying to us so we can provide them with the nourishment they need.

Here are 8 things that cause cravings and steps you can take to stop them:

1. **Lack of water or dehydration.** You may be craving a certain food when what you really need is water. Before you give in to that late afternoon snack, drink a big glass of water, wait a few minutes and see if you're still craving that food or whether you're really hungry at all.

2. **"Primary Food" deficit.** You are "malnourished" in another area of your life i.e career, family, sexuality, fitness. Have you ever noticed you may not want to eat that entire pint of ice cream when you're happy in your new relationship? Ask yourself what you need to fix in the circle you call your life.

3. **Yin/Yang imbalance.** Sometimes when you eat a certain kind of food it causes a craving for another type of food. For example, eating salty foods can cause a craving for sweet foods. Eating a lot of meat can cause a craving for alcohol. Check in to see if you are eating too much or not enough of a certain food group or if your diet is lacking in variety.

4. **Craving the foods of our ancestors.** Have you ever noticed that when you go back home to visit your family for a holiday or reunion, you start craving foods you would never eat in your own home?

   If you bring your partner, spouse or a friend with you on one of those trips, they may have a totally adverse reaction to those same foods! The foods your parents served to you during your childhood become part of your DNA. Next time you head back for a holiday dinner, note what feelings are associated with the foods that may be served. Do they comfort you? If so, why?

5. **Seasonal.** Do you notice when the weather starts getting warm, you crave more fruits, salads and raw foods? Then when the seasons start to move towards autumn and winter, you start to crave warmer foods like soups and root vegetables? These cravings are good cravings. Your body, if attuned, should start to anticipate and desire what the next harvest is bringing.

6. **Lack of nutrients.** When your body is out of balance, you may crave a certain food that will bring you back into balance. I was very lean when I got pregnant so during the first trimester of my pregnancy, my body needed to store fat to protect the fetus. I craved fatty foods like grilled cheese and fries. I put on 10 pounds within the first 8 weeks! My body knew what it had to do to prepare the womb for a baby to grow. Once my body was back in balance, I craved a healthy diet of fruits and vegetables again.

7. **Hormonal.** Most women know what it's like to crave certain foods around our menstrual cycles, or as I just stated above, during a pregnancy. These cravings are harder to stop since they are hormonal, but they, too, will pass.

8. **Eating foods with little nutritional value.** Products like refined foods, sugar, caffeine, alcohol and drugs, which have little or no nutritional value, are confusing to the body. They throw your body off balance and can create more serious cravings as your body tries to restore its internal harmony.

9. **Go without a certain food you crave** and want to remove from your diet for one month. Typically, after 3 weeks your body will stop craving it. This is perfect for items such as butter, salt, sweets.

My REAL education in food came after I attended IIN, the Institue for Integrative Nutrition, *www.IntegrativeNutrition.com*. It's a terrific institution, all online, and their approach is holistic. Check it out and email me at hayley@hayleyhobson.com if you, too, are interested in a career as a Health Coach.

Cravings will come and cravings will go. The key to stopping cravings is to understand them, not give in to them. Your diet may be too strict or devoid of essential nutrients. Your lifestyle may be too stressful.

You may need more exercise or more water. Ask yourself how you feel before you put something in your mouth and what you feel like after you eat it. As you learn to decipher and respond to your body's cravings, you will be able to create a diet and lifestyle that is more balanced.

When you think about stress or tension, where does your mind go?

Many of us think that stress is manifested in our physical bodies because we've just exercised. Maybe you have gone for a long run, or it's the first time you've exercised in awhile. Or, it could be due to a lack of activity, like sitting at a desk all day. Your muscles feel tight. There may be tension in your shoulders, neck or hips.

Very often it is our emotions that are wreaking havoc on our bodies much more than any amount of exercise we can do, and these emotions are stressing our internal organs. Do you ever notice how wrecked you feel after a fight you've had with your partner, after the death of a loved one, or after you've encountered some terrible news?

Or maybe sometimes it's anxiety over a situation at work or with your children that upsets you. Now the stress is manifesting itself in your digestive system. Symptoms can include bloating, gas, nausea or constipation. Your gut is literally telling you something is wrong.

When we feel stressed, we often reach for food that actually raises our anxiety levels. Coffee or other caffeinated beverages can seem appealing when you feel low. Sugary, processed foods or simple carbohydrates become our "comfort" foods. Unfortunately, these foods and beverages can make everything worse. Our liver goes into overdrive, we have trouble sleeping, and our symptoms increase.

So, what's the solution? Can we manage the disaster taking over our bodies? Yes! We have a choice in dealing with stress head on. The first step is to listen. What is your body saying to you? It's smarter than you think. The second step is to not ignore your symptoms anymore. Take initiative and move the stress out. The third step is to reach for food that actually lowers anxiety levels.

Here are a few foods that have been proven to lower stress levels:

1. **Blueberries:** The high potency of antioxidants in these berries counteracts the production of cortisol, the number one chemical that is released during a stressful time.

2. **Peaches:** This fruit is a fantastic super food. Peaches include phytonutrients that give you healthier skin and help fight cancer. They also have a natural sedative that can help reduce stress and anxiety. Plus, since they are sweet, they can work wonders when you need that sugary treat.

3. **Acacia berries:** This superfood should not be ignored. The acacia berry has phytonutrients that have been shown to enhance your mood. They have additional health benefits such as leveling your blood sugar which therefore reduces sugar cravings.

4. **Cacao:** Raw cacao is the ingredient found in chocolate. It is high in flavonoids. Flavonoids are potent with relaxation properties. Cacao also contains phenethylamine, a chemical that enhances mood. You can add raw cacao to your smoothies, your macaroons or you can get the nutrients by eating a dark chocolate bar. The darker the chocolate, the more of these substances you are getting. Generally, opt for bars with 70% cacao or higher.

5. **Maca root:** Maca root is a powder made from a Peruvian root and can be found in certain supplements and drink mixes. Maca root, in its unprocessed form, contains a phytonutrient that helps ward off anxiety and depression. Some studies have found that maca root is just as useful at fighting depression as prescription antidepressants since it contains so many mood enhancing nutrients.

Another plus is that maca root is natural and does not have as many of the risks or side effects of prescription anxiety medication. Maca root powder can be made into a tea or sprinkled over other foods to give you the maximum health benefits. You actually need very little. I add about a tablespoon to my smoothies.

6. **Spinach:** This lean, green leaf is high in magnesium, improves your body's overall response to stress and stops your blood pressure from spiking.

7. **Sunflower seeds:** Sunflower seeds contain a high source of folate, which helps your body produce the feel-good brain chemical dopamine. Normal levels of dopamine help control your emotional responses.

8. **Walnuts:** It has been shown that eating at least 1 ounce of walnuts a day can prevent your blood pressure from rising, and keep your anxiety levels in check. If you tend to have higher levels of adrenaline and anxiety, make sure you get some of these delicious nuts into your diet so you're not making your heart work more than it needs to. Walnuts can be a great addition to any salad or salad dressing.

These super foods are now everywhere if you know where to look. We are becoming more and more aware of our health and how what we eat affects our mood. If you have been feeling tension or stress, consider adding some of these super foods to your diet. They will have a calming effect on your body and help relieve feelings of anxiety.

Try using these super foods as alternatives for the more processed and less nutritious foods in your diet—particularly those high in fat, calories, and processed sugars. You won't believe the results.

At the beginning of last winter, I invited John Douillard to be the guest speaker for the Ayurvedic section of our YogaWorks teacher training.

Now I realize how lucky we were to have him spend part of the afternoon with us. After battling with intestinal dysfunction myself, and dealing with my children getting colds over and over again throughout the winter, I was fully absorbed by what he had to say. It's been almost a full year since his talk and his words have become a mantra I live by.

Have you ever noticed that with every season we get a new harvest? In the spring, we see a light harvest of bitter greens and vegetables (like kale and arugula.) In the summer, there is an abundance of cooling fruits (like mango and watermelon.) As we move towards winter, we see a heavier fall harvest of bananas, avocados and root vegetables like beets.

Although many people may stick to the same diet all year round, nature is speaking to us with each harvest. And we need to perk up our ears (and tummies) and listen! Our nutritional cycle in nature is an annual cycle. It actually takes an entire year for all of our nutritional needs to be met. Holistic health is all about preventing illness and injury before they happen, contrary to

typical Western medicine which prescribes to kill off symptoms. Prevention of our health issues takes weeks, months, and even a season or two prior to the event. For instance, cold and flu season prevention can go all the way back to the beginning of summer.

In the summertime, do you eat enough berries and cherries to cleanse your lymphatic system? If not, be sure you do!

Spring is the time to cleanse our bodies of all the excess mucus we've produced during winter.

It's the time to literally "clean out" and reset our metabolism so we'll be able to burn fat for energy during the summer. We should be eating a low fat diet of spring harvested fruits and vegetables like grapefruits, sprouts, bitter greens and light grains.

As summer approaches, we need foods that give us energy for the longer days and longer nights. We also need foods that are capable of cooling down our body temperatures. Our diets during this season should be 80% carbohydrates. Berries and cherries are optimal fruits in this season. These foods continue to scrape our intestinal walls and prepare us for the fall and winter.

Cherries are the last cleansing food before the fall harvest. After the cherries, the lymphatic cleansing benefits of nature are over! Say good-bye to summer picks, we're moving onto fall.

Fall is the time to flush our systems of the excess heat from summer. You'll notice you see more apples, pomegranates, beets and cranberries in your local markets. As we move into fall, we also need to store up fats and eat more protein in order to warm ourselves up for what lies ahead. The foods during the winter season are mucous-producing foods so we don't get so dried out in the winter.

Can you see the cycle?

And more importantly, can you follow it?

For more information about Hayley's Nutrition programs, visit **www.hayleyhobson.com**

7-Day DETOX

Last 5 lbs. in 14-Days

30-Day Flab to Fab

Chapter 2
YOGA SEQUENCE

1. SAVASANA
2. SUPTA HASTA PADDAHUSTASANA
3. ADHO MUKHA SVANASANA
4. LOW LUNGE
5. UTTANASANA
6. LOW LUNGE W/TWIST
7. RUNNERS LUNGE
8. ADHO MUKHA SVANASANA
9. HIGH PLANK
10. CHATTURANGA DANDASANA
11. URDHVA MUKHA SVANASANA
12. ADHO MUKHA SVANASANA
13. TRIKONASANA
14. PARSVAKONASANA
15. PARVRITTA TRIKONASANA
16. UTKATASANA W/TWIST
17. PARSVA BAKASANA
18. MALASANA
19. BADHA KONASANA
20. JANU SIRSASANA
21. MARICHYASANA C
22. SUPTA HASTA PADDAHASTASANA
23. SAVASANA

DETOX TWISTS

Visit **http://bit.ly/18w6vya** to access Hayley's downloadable Yoga class, *Core Yoga 4*.

Superfood Salad Madness

Ingredients

- 1 tbsp extra virgin olive oil
- 1 tbsp organic, brown mustard
- 1 tsp raw apple-cider vinegar
- pinch Himalayan Sea Salt and pepper
- 3 cups mixed shredded kale and red cabbage
- 1 carrot, peeled and julienned
- 1/4 cup fresh parsley leaves
- 2 tbsp diced red onion
- 2 tbsp sunflower seeds
- 2 tbsp pumpkin seeds
- 2 tbsp hemp seeds

Instructions

In a small bowl, whisk extra virgin olive oil, mustard, and apple-cider vinegar. Season with Himalayan Sea Salt and pepper. In another bowl, combine kale, cabbage, carrot, parsley and red onion with sunflower, pumpkin and hemp seeds. Season with Himalayan Sea Salt and pepper, drizzle with dressing, and toss to coat.

Green Banana Smoothie

Ingredients

- 1 banana
- 1/2 pineapple
- 1 cup coconut milk
- handful of shredded coconut
- 1 heaping spoonful of green powder
- handful of spinach
- handful of kale
- 1 tbsp of raw organic honey

Instructions

Mix in blender.

Nutrients:
Beta-carotene, folic acid, Vitamins B1, B3, B6; calcium, magnesium, manganese, phosphorus, potassium, sodium, sulphur, protein, essential fatty acids.

This smoothie is great for energy and digestion.

~ Chapter 3 ~
EXERCISE

I WAS 5 YEARS OLD AND DYING TO GET MY EARS PIERCED.

My mother promised me my wish if I was able to swim 2 lengths of the 25-meter pool at our swim club and tread water for two minutes on my own. Even at that age, nothing could stand in the way of my true hearts desire. By the middle of the summer I was sporting my little 14-carat gold posts and I was the youngest swimmer on our team.

By age 8, I was swimming the 25-meter butterfly in our tri-county championships and every year after, I was on the winning age-group relay. I swam competitively through high school and when I moved to Los Angeles in the mid 90's and the incredible weather took me outdoors more than ever before, I fell in love with running and cycling. With my swimming background, I became a natural at the sport of triathlon until numerous injuries and accidents forced me to reexamine my obsessive need to train every day, oftentimes more than once.

Since then, I've started my own business and have a family to take care of. Long gone are the days when I had the luxury of exercising as much as I used to. However, I still make myself several promises—I will never let more than 2 days go by without exercising, I will always push myself past my comfort zone and I will always give myself a pat on the back just for making the time to get out there and do it. It is my hope that after reading this chapter, you will find the same inspiration to get out there and get your juices flowing!

Rising to the Challenge.

5:30am. My alarm is going off. It's so tempting to stay buried underneath the covers. Why am I getting up at this ungodly hour in the dark...when it's getting colder and colder out...to meet this insane group of runners that band together every Tuesday, Friday and Sunday?

Our coach sends us the workouts a month in advance but I usually don't look at them ahead of time. I don't want to stress myself out with the session he's got in store for us.

I'd much rather get a good night's sleep and then be shocked when I meet them all in the morning.

This morning it was a 4-mile tempo run up Flagstaff mountain. Do you have any idea what it feels like to run uphill, starting at 5600 feet above sea level and then gain another 1000 feet by the time you reach the top? Awful. Yes. Awful. On top of it, I'm the oldest one in the group by at least 10 years and the slowest one in the group by far.

With that said, I love my running group. The first day I showed up to meet this group I got smoked. I am not talking by a lap, I'm talking

"I will never grow if I stay in my comfort zone."

roadrunner style: *beep, beep, bye-bye.* Most people probably would have walked away with their tail between their legs, quit, or searched out an old ladies' running group. Instead I rose to the occasion, stepped up to the challenge and kept at it, knowing I could use these women and their speed as a way to push myself to a level I may never get to by myself.

One of the mantras I live by is "I will never grow if I stay in my comfort zone." It takes guts and courage to run in the first place. Circumstances such as family, work and time can always get in the way and be used as an excuse. This running team is made up of elite athletes a decade or more younger than me! I am not a slow runner, by any means, but these women crush it, sometimes out-running me by a couple of laps around the track. I'm talking regional and national championship level. So, I ask myself several days a week, "What am I doing here?"

In difficult moments, it's so easy to give up or at least to want to give up. Wouldn't it be easier to pull those covers over my head and go back to sleep? Go for an easier run on my own? Or not push the pace as hard as I feel compelled to when I'm with these women? Of course! It's in these moments of weakness that I need to accept the challenge and go past where I thought I could ever go.

I'd love to tell you that all it takes is an act of will, but that's simply not true. Pushing

yourself in any capacity requires heart, determination and discipline. In theory, we all have heart—it's the determination and discipline we must discover within ourselves so that we can see what it will take to go beyond our comfort zone.

There have been so many occasions I have wanted to quit. I would tell myself the story that I was in the wrong group, I could find an easier team... As time went on and my speed began to increase, I was still getting crushed. Although I don't consider myself a glutton for punishment, I pushed on. I knew if I wanted to grow, it meant gravitating towards people who are where I desire to be at some point.

I feel better about myself when I know I am challenged. I am a human being filled with potential, a potential I may never live to see uncovered or experienced if I don't pursue my dreams. I need to know what I am capable of, what I am made of and how far I can go if I follow my heart.

For those of you thinking about joining a group yourself, wanting to raise the bar in your own life and challenge yourself to function and perform at your optimum level, here are a few thoughts you can process:

- You won't know what you can or cannot do until you give it a try.

- If you feel like quitting, trust that you are not the only person who feels or has ever felt this way.

- Have patience and be kind to yourself. Rome was not built in one day. You will get faster if you show up and do your workouts.

Don't compare yourself to anyone else but yourself. You are not how fast you are, how thin you are, what kind of car you are driving or what job you hold. Notice your accomplishments and give yourself a pat on the back.

Getting smoked and feeling like a slow poke doesn't exactly invite warm feelings into my being, but I try to keep my intentions in perspective and not allow my ability to get sabotaged by my ego.

Running is exhilarating to me and if it weren't for this group I'm running with right now, I would never be the runner I am today. Nor would I be able to share this act of humility with you and encourage those of you in my shoes to rise to the challenges that confront you in life. You may surprise yourself and find that you are much stronger and more capable than you ever thought you were.

There will always be someone faster, stronger, smarter, or prettier.

The question is: where do you want to be and what steps will you take to be the best that you can be? If something is still holding you back, kick it to the curb, put your running shoes on and get out the door.

At least you're out there.

Yoga: More than a cute butt and flat abs...

Admit it. You attended your first yoga class because you wanted that cute butt and tight torso. It's okay, we all thought about it at one point. When I started practicing in my early 20s, I believed yoga would be a great pathway to keeping me slim and fit. Oh, and then supposedly, I'd become more virtuous and calm down too? I liked the idea of myself as a yoga person. I began to eat, sleep and dream yoga.

From Downward Dog to Triangle Pose, I was drawn in. Absorbed. By the time I lay down, a sweaty mess in Savasana, I was—do I dare to say—"blissed out?" There were 80 other sweaty strangers in the room with me, (even touching me) and I didn't mind at all! I began to wonder what it was about this practice that was bringing me to such a state of calm and serenity. Why was it that the entire room was falling into a zen-like atmosphere and no one wanted to leave?

My instructor would walk around the room, slowly, with a sense of earthly groundedness and I'd begin to wonder, mid-Camel Pose, "How can it be that he moves with such poise and grace?" As I followed my teacher's cues and did my work to the best of my ability, I began to reap the benefits of my practice.

It took me awhile but I eventually did realize there was much more to the practice than planking until my abs and arms were toned to the MAX. Submission, trust, imperfection, letting go of fear and the release of ego were some of the initial attributes I began to realize. As I began to shift into new shapes, I derived more and more pleasure in becoming someone new, off my mat.

I didn't realize the shift was coming. It just sort of snuck up on me. Have you noticed that yourself? Even if you, too, began your practice for the perks of becoming more toned or flexible, something has shifted. The real perk has become how flexible your mind has become. For whatever reason any of us has landed in yoga class, ultimately we all begin to walk down a path closer to enlightenment.

I wanted to bring that zen and awe-inspiring serenity into my own home. I didn't need to have to go only to the studio. It needed to become my life. How did I do it? ***PRACTICE.***

The roots of Yoga go back to over 5,000 years ago. Yikes! That was a long time ago! Why did it take so long to get to the United States? It started in Northern India as a way to rejuvenate the body and prolong life. It was also used to deepen the physical-spiritual connection we all have within us.

Yoga comes from the Sanskrit word "yuj," which means to "yoke" or "unite." You can see "it's" more than what most American yogis think "it" is; "it's" about the "coming together" within all of this. Yoga helps us take a look at all aspects of our lives… pleasure and pain, joy and misery, and nudges us to accept all parts. We live in a crazy and intense world. As such, we've become far too distracted. It's too easy to lose touch with ourselves and our lives. Yoga is a path to get back in balance (no pun intended!)

Through the physical asanas, we gain clarity of mind which allows us to unite with all parts of ourselves in order to feel peace. It's a way to brush away distractions, imperfections, and ignorance in order to see the part each one of us plays in the universe itself, bonded with all creatures. It's a pretty *crazy-amazing* feeling once you reach that point of understanding.

Too heavy for you? No worries. In time, as you continue to practice—whether you want to or not—you will begin to tune in. Your yoga practice will become much more than a means to a cute butt and flat abs. You'll start to see your place in the world around you in a completely different way. Trust me; your life too will change for the better.

Perfection in the Pilates Studio.

Last week I was witness to a breakdown. However, instead of it being my 3-year-old daughter, it was one of my longtime Pilates students.

I was moving my client through a classically choreographed session on the reformer when suddenly, we got to Short Spine, usually everyone's favorite exercise and she stopped and cried, "I shouldn't be doing this! Nothing I'm doing is ever right!"

I was startled. I knew this client well. She had made so much progress in her body, and while observing her technique, the thought that had actually been going through my mind was, "Wow! She is really connecting." Where was this coming from?

"I'm not getting better, Hayley. I'll never make any progress."

Chloe had been showing up weekly for privates and classes for well over a year. In my eyes, she had made tremendous progress. She originally came in almost limping in pain and since that first day she had strengthened her core, gained lots of flexibility in her hamstrings, hips and spine, toned her arms, improved her balance, and is totally pain-free. Movements that had once been a challenge for her were now

a piece of cake. Exercises that once left her out of breathe now barely made her break a sweat. She had become a smooth, coordinated, and well-oiled machine.

However, in Chloe's eyes, she was unable to see any progress. Instead, she had been taking corrections as negative feedback and honestly believed she had to move perfectly or else she was not doing it "right."

What Chloe did not understand was that the Pilates Method, like any other Mind/Body regime, was a practice. No one is ever going to be perfect, and no matter how much progress a student is ever making, I feel obliged, as her instructor, to challenge just a bit more.

There is always room for transformation in our bodies. And if you don't believe this, or don't want to be challenged, why practice at all? Practice allows us to gain a much more multifaceted connection to our bodies. If we cannot make profound connection to ourselves, how are we able to have compassion for anyone else around us? If we are not challenged, we will never change.

Don't you want to be a better version of yourself today than you were yesterday?

What Chloe most likely did not realize was that during each of her sessions, the cues I gave her became increasingly sophisticated. What I was saying to her today was information her brain would not be able to digest in our first lesson.

Now, after time and a dedicated practice, Chloe's mind AND body are able to have a more intelligent conversation with each other. She is capable of being pushed to a much deeper level than she could have been pushed even a few short months ago. It often takes someone else's guidance to give ourselves the little nudge we need — the nudge that sends us along the path we've always intended.

My client Chloe was not seeing the road she'd come down. She was frustrated. Every time she came in, she felt like she was still struggling. Was she resisting moving outside of her comfort zone because she wanted to excel, to succeed, to look good? Did she want to be perfect at her Pilates practice, just like she strove to be the perfect wife, the perfect mother and the perfect employee in her office?

If Chloe was striving for perfection, she'd never find it in my Pilates studio. Pilates isn't something we can check off a list. I've practiced Pilates for 15 years and I still don't feel like I've mastered it. I continue to work. I continue to practice. I continue to soar towards reaching new heights. I continue to evolve both in my practice and in my life. In fact, I often see my

practice as the metaphor for my life. I reassured Chloe that was she doing beautifully and reminded her that what we had done today she couldn't do a year ago, or even 6 months ago. Eventually she smiled. "You're right. Let's keep going."

Finding your ideal anatomical posture can be difficult.

We never really know what we look like unless we're literally looking in the mirror. Have you ever been in a yoga class, thought you were in a pose exactly the way your teacher was cueing it and when he or she came around and adjusted you, it felt like you were going to fall over? I know. I've been there too. It's called *hanging out in our imbalances.* To most of us, "being" in ideal anatomical alignment is actually a lot of work.

Let's face it, we've done a lot of work over the course of our lifetimes to bring ourselves out of alignment, whether that be years of sitting at a computer, huddled forward on our iPhones or video games, or even rounded forward on a bicycle. Our bodies have gotten a beating and our muscles have begun to pull on our bones in a way that is....let's say....not so pretty.

So here you go. A little drill in standing up straight. I bet if you work it, you'll actually feel like you're giving yourself a "workout!"

1. Stand with your legs hip distance apart. Find the four corners of your feet—ball mound of the big toe, ball mound of the little toe and the inner and outer heel equally descending into the ground. Once you feel grounded in your feet, lift your toes to engage your arches to create a muscular energy in the soles of your feet. Now, hug your shins into the midline and notice how your inner thighs turn on and the muscular energy moves towards your midline.

2. Once your shins are hugging in, energetically rotate your inner thighs back and apart in order to hollow your groins and widen your sacrum. If this is difficult for you to find, put a yoga block in-between your upper thighs and push the block backwards. Notice how you may feel less tension in your poses and crease of your hips. With your inner thighs back and apart, drop your tailbone down towards the floor and curl it in, ever so slightly towards your pubic bone so your pelvis moves more towards a neutral position. You may feel your low belly muscles wake up and your frontal hip bones lift up.

3. Now that you are firmly rooted, you will have a sense of groundedness or support from which you can expand through your upper body and open your chest. Lift the sides of your body up. Imagine someone is lifting your armpits or upper arm bones up. Then, take the top of your arm bones back. Can you picture your shoulder blades? Press the bottom tips of your shoulder blades up and into your chest. Can you feel the mini backbend sneaking up on you without anyone else noticing? This shoulder blade "mantra" are words of alignment to live by and the keys to open up your heart.

4. With your upper body expanding, you may feel like you are popping your ribs out. So use your third chakra energy to pull that power right back into you. Yes, pull your ribs back with your abdominals! If you're shoulders came off your back, use your shoulder blade mantra again. I know what you're thinking but no one said this was going to be easy! Just standing up requires work. Now when you go into your yoga class or any activity you do, you'll have a place to start in every pose.

5. Once you've got your upper body in check, you may feel like you've lost your legs and pelvis. Not to worry. Just start all over. Continue to scan you body up and down, down and up. Just like that, whether your standing in a yoga class, in the grocery store or even on an airplane, you are giving yourself a mini workout and the key to your most excellent posture.

Chapter 3
YOGA SEQUENCE

1. SUKASANA
2. SUKASANA W/UTTITA HASTA ARMS
3. SUKASANA SEATED SIDE BENDS
4. SUKASANA W/ARMS CLASPED OVERHEAD - SIDEBENDS
5. SUKASANA W/ARMS REACHING FORWARD
6. SUKASANA W/ARMS CLASPED BEHIND BACK
7. NAVASANA
8. LOLASANA
9. ADHO MUKHA SVANASANA
10. PLANK
11. ADHO MUKHA SVANASANA
12. HALF SUN SALUTE
13. LOW LUNGES
14. VIRABHADRASANA I
15. VRKASANA
16. HANDSTAND WITH FEET AT WALL
17. HANDSTAND
18. PADAHASTASANA
19. HALASANA
20. SALAMBA SARVANGASANA
21. MATSYASANA
22. SIMPLE TWIST
23. SAVASANA

INVERSION ELEMENT SEQUENCE

11

16

21

12

HALF SUN
SALUTE

SEE PAGE 12

17

22

13

18

23

14

19

Visit **http://bit.ly/TkejNJ**
to access Hayley's downloadable
Yoga class, *Tighten Your Core.*

15

20

Chapter 3
RECIPES

Mega Antioxidant Juice

Ingredients

- 1 grapefruit
- 2 oranges
- 3 carrots
- 1 inch ginger root
- 1 drop Ginger essential oil
- 1 drop Orange essential oil
- 1 drop Grapefruit essential oil

Instructions

Juice all together in your juicer. Add 1 drop of each of the essential oils.

One of the first things I like to do each morning is **JUICE** so I get fresh nutrients and live enzymes into my body first thing. When the cold and flu season hits, this is one of my favorite recipes packed with beta carotene and antioxidants to ward off those unnecessary evils.

> "Cooking is like love, it should be entered with abandon or not at all."
>
> ~HARRIET VAN HORNE

More than Quinoa Cereal

Ingredients

- 1 cup quinoa
- 1/4 cup hemp milk
- 1 tbsp sesame seed butter
- 1 tbsp raw, organic honey
- 1 tsp cinnamon
- 1 drop Cinnamon essential oil

Instructions

1. Heat water to boil.
2. Pour quinoa into boiling water.
3. Cover and turn stove to simmer for 15-20 min.
4. Once all water is evaporated and quinoa is light, remove from stove and place in bowl.
5. Pour hemp milk in bowl with quinoa and stir until desired consistency.
6. Add sesame butter, organic honey and cinnamon.

This is a simple, healthy cereal that you can make and use for a whole week!

~ Chapter 4 ~
RELATIONSHIPS

DO YOU REMEMBER THAT SEINFELD EPISODE from ages ago where Jerry, Elaine, George and Kramer all had plans to go to a movie but no one had made the time or location clear? They each left their respective apartments to search for one another but never united. Can you imagine that happening today? Of course not! There would have been dozens of text messages sent back and forth until they were all sitting quietly in the theater together. In fact, that show would never even have existed in our world today. Why? Because it was built around the idea of relationships and people sitting around doing nothing but talking to each other! A rare situation in the world of technology in which we now live.

Technology has become a "more than significant" part of our lives. Wherever I go, I see dozens of people with their heads deep in iPhones or alternative mobile devices. It doesn't matter if they are on the subway, waiting in line at the market or out to dinner with others. Phones are in tow and always on.

We email rather than call. We send text messages more often than we need to. What happened to the idea of quality time with those we love? In this chapter, I want to remind you to take notice of those around you. To appreciate all the gifts they have to offer. To love and cherish every moment you have with them—even if it's not for long. And to say "thank you," "I'm sorry," "I understand you," and "I love you."

Here's the deal. We are all caught up in the craziness we call life.

Our world has gotten so fast-paced, so intense and so insane, it is hard just to keep up on a daily basis. There are days I feel like a hamster doing a dance on her wheel, merely in an attempt to stay in one place and not fall backwards. What's the trick? How can we manage everything on our plates so our lives don't literally take us down? It's no big secret. We've just got to tune in and LISTEN TO OUR BODIES. It often takes incidents like this for me to learn my own lesson.

Every few weeks it seems like there is a day (or more) that my daughter, Madeline's preschool is closed. Last spring, when she was almost three, a full week closure posed an interesting situation for me. I am a full-time working mom. Madeline is in school Monday through Friday so that I can run my company. My first thought, when I remembered the staff in-service days was, "I can totally do this. She is at such a fun age right now and has no problem occupying herself." Anyone smirking already?

I had scheduled several Pilates and yoga clients throughout the day and really thought I'd be able to put Madeline in front of her favorite TV show, *Mickey Mouse Clubhouse*, while I taught the

sessions. Since all of my other meetings are held on line or over the phone, I figured I could easily deal with her while I took care of business. Over 100 emails in my inbox, which is the norm every day? No biggie. We could hang together while I responded. WHO WAS I KIDDING?

All day long, Madeline was attached to me like a barnacle. She was so excited to be home with her mommy that she could not peel herself off of my body. "Uppie," she cried out to me all day long. That's code for "Although I normally am able to walk around all day long without you, since you are letting me stay home with you, I am unable to find the strength to stand on my own two feet today."

And the few times I left her alone even for a few moments, I either found her 1) on top of the kitchen countertop eating her entire jar of vitamins; 2) smearing a tube of toothpaste all over her brand new life-sized Mickey Mouse because, don't you know, he needs to brush his teeth too; or 3) drawing with permanent marker in my closet on the walls. And remember, she was out of school for a week.

So, needless to say, I rarely had a minute to myself. She was whispering in my ear that she needed her "wadah," "cwackahs," "ceweal and gogurt," and other treats that didn't always exist. If she didn't get them instantaneously, she had a fit. And when she was in a good mood (ah, the mood swings of a 3-year-old), she had a dire need to show me her Sesame Street stuffed animals and her "Loving Family People" from her dollhouse. I was always a constant necessity for her. The space I needed, between her and my work, was crashing into nothingness and I felt myself beginning to crack.

Still, as a good American and nonstop mother, I pressed on, not listening to what my body was saying to me. By 5pm Thursday afternoon, my stomach was in knots, my stress levels roaring out of control, and I felt myself beginning to break down. A scheduled call came in, and with whatever remaining level of calm I had left in my body, I let the person on the other end know that it was not going to happen until my husband came home from work and peeled my darling daughter off of me.

When my husband finally walked in the door at 6pm, I was relieved to finally get some space. I just needed to sit, breathe some air that wasn't from my daughter's requests or complaints, and inhale the me. Warm bath, essential oils, relaxing book, good night sleep. I figured I'd be fine in the morning.

We've got to tune in and listen to our bodies.

...it is an absolute must to keep listening to your body with a highly tuned ear—to prevent stress, injuries, and disease.

Daddy was on duty. I woke up at 5:45am to get together with my running team at the track. I was moving so slow, just getting my shoes on made me weary about the proceeding hours of exercise. I did a simple loop around the high school to warm up. My normal expected warm up pace is, at the most, 8 minutes. This first loop was predicting at least a 12-minute mile. I just couldn't get my body going fast enough! I knew the stress was eating at my insides.

Finally, I perked up, listened to my body, and got back in the car. There was no way I was going to be able to do the session. I fell into bed and slept for two hours. I couldn't eat solid food for the next 48 hours. Here it goes again.

What was wrong with me? My body was SHOUTING at me! Stress! When was I going to finally learn my lesson? I continued a cycle of relaxation, hydration and peace, resulting in my body releasing its tension and finally getting back to normal.

Moral of the story: LISTEN TO YOUR BODY.

After years of ignoring my body's cries for help, I finally realized the never-give-up attitude isn't always the best. It's hard to slow it down when you're ambitious and highly driven like me, but if you keep going at that pace, you'll be sure to drive yourself into the ground at some point. When the unexpected happens, you need to have the tools to prepare for such an event. While being well-nourished and having a healthy mind are the best battle tactics against a stress-filled world, it is an absolute must to keep listening to your body with a highly tuned ear—to prevent stress, injuries and disease.

Preventive action is what's important here—not action *when it is too late.* Is it really worth it to do that extra run if it costs you days of being flat on your back in bed? Did it really make sense for me to think I could work full time all week when little Madeline was home all day?

I'm always in the process of learning and now I know—next time there is a school closure, it means time off for me too! I'll be canceling clients and taking some personal time. I'll be laying off my heavy work schedule to better balance the time with my daughter.

None of us needs to be Superwoman—if we are smarter and more well-balanced, we won't fall into the trap of being over-stressed to the breaking point. Furthermore, I'll never get that time with Madeline back so it's worth it to me.

I now see those in-school closures as a gift from God. And at least I'll know she isn't digesting 3 packs of chewing gum when I'm in the other room on the phone.

I used to feel like my family might as well be eating SPAM for dinner.

I'd look over at my husband's plate: two hearty mounds of meatloaf and not a vegetable in sight. Then my daughter's predictable plate: goat's milk yogurt, gluten-free cereal, maybe dried mangos and gluten-free pretzels. She only eats 5 things. Total. *Awesome, right?* I guess I can use the excuse that she's three.

Then there is my plate: a mélange of assorted raw vegetable salads. As I would sit there, I would find myself confounded by the "funny food farm" on our dining room table.

Eating well is not just some sidebar of my character; it's an integral aspect of who I am. I walk the talk. I talk the walk. Good nutrition and healthy eating habits for me are essential. It's nonnegotiable. So how come I couldn't get my family to eat anything that wasn't processed and out of a box? They wanted nothing to do with my plate. My husband would see green and ask where the main course was. My daughter would see green and ask for her crackers.

It was maddening. Do you feel like you're in the same boat? Are you struggling to teach your family to be conscientious of what they put inside their bodies? Are you trying to align your family's eating habits with your own values when they clearly don't care?

Let me tell you, this is not an easy task. Converting your family to a conscious nutrition program takes education and time. Bad habits are hard to break. I know—I had my bad habits too. Ultimately, for me, there was no other choice. My digestive system went haywire! I was at the end of my rope and unwilling to feel less than perfect anymore.

The strange thing is, most people have accepted less than optimal digestion. Gas, bloating, constipation, fatigue, moodiness, sluggishness and terrible sleeping patterns have become the norm and no one looks to their diets as the potential cause.

These symptoms do not have to be acceptable. Not for you and not for your family. So, how do you change their eating habits without feeling like the Evil Grinch?

- **Make it fun.** Bring your kids into the kitchen with you to prepare their own food. When they have a chance to be included in the experience, they may want to eat what they've prepared. My three year old knows how to use our juicer and my 11 year old loves using the Cuisinart. She even bought me a dehydrator for Christmas last year!

- **"Sneak" veggies into their food.** There are ways to create delicious green smoothies with enough fruit in them so their picky taste buds still enjoy.

- **Make sure your kiddos are on a multi-vitamin, bi-omegas and active calcium.** Even with the diet I have, I consider supplementation a necessity. Unless your kids are eating 10 pounds of spinach a day and 15 cans of sardines, chances are, they too need supplementation.

- **Try a variety of new recipes.** For your man who won't eat his veggies, instead of overhauling his eating habits, create the kind of salads or vegetable dishes that you think he may love. Experiment. Get online or check out my **blog** to find recipes that spruce up your standard vegetables. He too will start to crave them in their raw form like you do. You can also start making killer salads that incorporate tons of great things he'll love. A chopped salad with romaine, salami, feta cheese, apple, carrots, cucumber, finely chopped kale, nuts, bell pepper and avocado, tossed in an apple cider vinegar and olive oil based dressing will convert any man.

If you're tired of your family's eating habits and concerned with their general health and well-being, you are going to have to take control. Grab the bull by the horns, and experiment in a way that makes your family members feel good about your choices—and theirs.

You may have to fly in under the radar instead of banging them over the head with accusations about how ridiculous their eating habits may seem to you, but if you are willing to put in the effort and remember to keep it fun and positive, you too will be able to inspire your family to make better choices. Soon, you'll be hearing your kids asking if they can help you prepare a salad or better yet, your hubby ordering a vegetarian meal when you go out to eat!

A few days ago, I woke up with a stifling headache.

I never get headaches. For quite some time I walked around with this throbbing pain in my head, until I was able to unload onto one of my girlfriends something that had been upsetting me for days. After I was able to vent, I realized that this headache had manifested in my body due to the stress of the situation I'd been obsessing about. If I hadn't been able to feel heard, and process what I'd been holding onto all week, the tension in my head most likely would have continued to exasperate.

Life is so hectic and busy that sometimes we're unaware of how afflicted we are by the stresses of our lives. We are so programmed to 'keep it together' and pretend that we don't experience things to the depth we do at times. It's only when we have a platform to express our feelings that we understand what is going on within. No one in the world will listen to you and help you through the trenches of life's murky waters like your girlfriends.

Girlfriends are the bread and butter of our sanity. Whether you realize it or not, women need other women. We all need to unleash and feel heard. A true girlfriend will listen to you, be your cheerleader when you need one, tell you to get your sh*t together when you're out of control and let you know when you can't pull off the outfit you're wearing anymore.

No one understands the mama drama we go through, frustrations with the opposite sex, or trials and tribulations, like 'the girls.'

So if having women in our lives is important why does it often seem so difficult to get together with our friends in a meaningful way? How do we get quality 'girl time' when life is so busy?

Men tend to process their inner world in a solitary way. Women, however, need to find outlets to stop the endless chatter in our brains. Our girlfriends provide that outlet in ways that our husband, boyfriends or partners cannot. Our partners may be listening to our "noise," but sometimes I feel that all they hear is Charlie Brown's mom—*wha wha wha wha wha wha*—in the background. Yep, that's

exactly what we sound like to them. When we talk, the men may ignore us because they can't deal or they go into Mr. Fix It mode, wanting to solve our problems instead of just listening. Girlfriends can provide an ear and a little compassion.

Here's the deal. If we want to have meaningful relationships with our girlfriends we need to make it a priority. We need to schedule it. And then—not flake. I know. It sounds so basic, but it's not for most people. It's easy to find a thousand reasons not to make the effort or to allow other things to take precedence. By "scheduling girl time" I don't mean connecting on your morning jog, or when you're racing to catch up with each other, or attending a yoga class together.

I mean make time.

Here are five virtually effortless ways to make your relationship with the women you love in your life a priority:

1. **Girls Nights Out** - the perfect way to catch up with those closest to you. Create a special time to get dressed up, feel beautiful and go out for a night on the town with just the girls! It's so fun— you need it!

2. **Meet for lunch or tea** - another fantastic way to get girl time. One hour of tea time can often be the remedy you need to catch up.

3. **Ever heard of Chick Swap?** It's where you take all the clothes you don't want or wear anymore, gather all your female companions, unload and trade your threads. The clothes you may not want in your closet anymore could be exactly what your BFF has been looking for and vice versa!

4. **Make plans with your girlfriend** to attend a book reading or seminar on something uber-inspiring and then discuss afterward at your favorite sushi or raw food restaurant. This is a great evening to share your inspirations.

5. **Throw a theme party** - nothing brings the girls together like costumes and party favors. Dancing, laughing, having a ball. Sign me up!

Bottom line: Girlfriends are the air we breathe. They make our lives a thousand times better and anything that makes our lives better is worth investing in and creating time for. As a life practice I am devoted to doing what makes me feel good.

Girlfriends are just as important as anything else in life. Sitting for tea or lunch might be too much for most people with jammed packed lives, but where there is a will there is a way. Don't cheat yourself on girlfriend time. Honor how good it makes you feel to cultivate those relationships and make it a priority. You need it and so does your girlfriend. Give her a call.

Last year I was back East visiting my parents for a few days when my mother and I got into one of our not so unusual spats.

I love my mother more than I can articulate, but we get into arguments every once in a while that leave us on non-speaking terms for days. Not good. It usually ruins our stay together and I end up feeling like a train wreck. Words go back and forth that neither one of us intended and when the argument is over, neither one of us can even remember how it began. We are out of alignment, and if I'm out of alignment with even one person in my life, I feel out of alignment with the entire universe.

Have you ever said something that was either so ridiculous or so spiteful that you wish you could take it back? Of course you have. I know I have. Too many times. We all become monsters of our madness at certain times in our lives. Our stress can definitely get the best of us. With so much going on around us every minute in this very intense and competitive world we live in, it's easy to see why we may react without thoughtfulness.

However, as crazy as our lives may be, there is absolutely no excuse for atrocious behavior. So, what's the best way to prevent yourself from becoming a crazy person... from saying things that you don't really mean? How do you prevent yourself from

sticking your foot in your mouth to begin with so you never have to eat your words?

1. **Zip It!** When you are frustrated or upset, walk away!

2. **24-Hour Rule** - Do not respond to anyone or any situation that is going to make you sound like a crazy person within at least 24 hours. As one of my mentors, Maria Forleo says, "Check yourself before you wreck yourself."

3. **Breathe!** - When you get upset, your stress levels rise even more and you may find you are not even breathing. Inhale long and deep. Exhale all the air out.

Sounds like a plan, right? Yes, in an ideal world you would never again say anything inappropriate. Realistic? No, of course not. You will always have your not-so-perfect days and something yucky will unintentionally slip out. So what do you do?

Be proactive and clean it up! There is nothing better than an apology. It is the glue that brings all the pieces back together. I cannot think of any circumstance where an apology was inappropriate. It can repair pretty much anything so long as it's sincere. So even if you feel self-conscious (which you should), make the approach and say you are sorry.

So, who are you writing your 'I'm sorry letter' to now? I know I'm going to call my mom just to tell her I love her.

Going home for the holidays is always loaded and laden with mixed emotions.

Most of us these days do not live close to our immediate families, and holidays may be the only time we see our parents and siblings all year. So, while there may be a level of excitement that comes with heading "home," if your family is like mine, having all the siblings and children under one roof can potentially cause a lot of stress.

I was looking forward to flying down to Florida last year for Thanksgiving. My parents love to see all of their grandchildren and it's a bonus that the weather is usually beautiful so my little ones can play in the pool or on the beach. However, once my sister and brother arrived with their significant others and their children, my parents' cozy home soon became as crazy as the Bronx Zoo. This holiday was no different than any of the rest. The melodrama had begun.

My mother is a clean freak. My husband will tell you that I've inherited this trait, as I can't stand having one thing out of order in my house, but my mother is the queen of obsessive compulsiveness. I kid you not when I say I would have no problem eating off of her floors. This week was no different. The moment we came in from a run or woke up in the morning, she asked us for the clothes off our back so she could wash them. I shouldn't complain, right? It's always nice to go home without one piece of dirty laundry in my suitcase... But for some reason, this time, it really started to bother me; she couldn't relax. I could see how all that tension was shattering her nerves. I kept telling her we'd wash our own clothes, but she was relentless. The obsessiveness continued to escalate. We couldn't leave our purses on her counters, our iPhones on her tables, eat in any room but her kitchen without her organizing their placement within minutes. God forbid we walk into the house with or shoes on. And if I expressed my desire to make a meal, she had a panic attack that her kitchen would actually get dirty.

Then there was my brother-in-law. He is always on his own time schedule. He wakes up when he wants, oblivious to the fact that it may be almost midday. If he's asked to arrive at noon for lunch, he shows up at 1:30pm. You can definitely say he's drumming to his own beat!

My sister is the princess of beauty products. She is never seen without mascara or a tinted moisturizer. She is constantly lusting after the newest beauty products on the market and arrived this time with a slew of products she wanted to apply on my face. I told you we were at the beach, right? Although her face always looks perfect, I prefer a more natural look and rarely wear much makeup.

Just as my sister was pushing her product on me, I was becoming relentless in the kitchen. The diet my family is used to eating is just not my cup of tea. I arrived, fully prepared with my juicer, and headed to the grocery store straight away to ensure I was fully stocked. I prepared every single meal separately from the ones they were preparing and am certain I turned them into closet eaters all week. I'm sure they were relieved upon my departure so they could go back to eating all the meat, dairy and Doritos they normally included in their diets.

We all have our traits and habits that make up our genetic structure. As quirky as they are, these traits are what make us who we are. The truth? Nothing any of us was doing was hurting anybody else. So instead of being bothered at my mother's insistence that every child make up his or her bunk bed in the morning, I reminded myself to celebrate what makes her unique and different. Maybe folding laundry all day is as therapeutic to her as heading out for a run is to me.

As we packed up the car to head to the airport, I got teary that I wouldn't see my family again until spring break in March. Annoying traits and all, I love them unconditionally. Don't forget to relax and enjoy every crazy quirk about each member of your family. They are the only family you have.

Chapter 4
YOGA SEQUENCE

1. ACTIVE LISTENING
2. ACTIVE TOUCH
3. GROUNDING WITH PARTNER
4. BALANCE
5. TRUST
6. SUPPORTED HEART OPENER
7. ALIGNING WITH ENERGY
8. CREATIVE ROOTING
9. OPENING WITH ACKNOWLEDGEMENT
10. FREEDOM
11. COMPASSION
12. SURRENDER

PARTNER YOGA

Visit **http://bit.ly/10x3VFF** to access Hayley's downloadable Yoga class, *HardCORE Pilates*.

Chapter 4
RECIPES

Spicy "Szechuan" Noodles

Ingredients

- 2 Zucchinis
- 1 Carrot
- 1 Bok Choy, separated
- Snap Peas, diced
- 1 Broccoli floret, chopped
- 2 Red Hot Chili Peppers
- Sunflower sprouts (handful)
- Bean sprouts (handful)
- Alfalfa sprouts (handful)
- Black sesame seeds

For the Dressing:

- 1/2 lime
- 1/2 cup olive oil
- 1 tbsp sesame oil
- 3-4 tbsp curry powder
- pinch of sea salt to taste
- 1 tbsp agave sweetener
- Cayenne pepper to taste

Instructions

Spiralize the zucchini into pasta-like noodles. Grate carrots. Chop all other vegetables.

For the Dressing:

Whisk all dressing ingredients together and pour over noodles. Sprinkle sesame seeds on top. Enjoy!

Coconut Almond Macaroons

Ingredients

- 1 cup dried, shredded coconut
- 1/2 cup tahini
- 1/2 cup almond butter or ground almonds
- 1/2 cup agave
- 2 tsp vanilla extract

Instructions

In a bowl, combine coconut, tahini, agave nectar, almond butter and vanilla. Using your hands, work together until well incorporated. If mixture is not incorporating, add more tahini.

Using a spoon or ice cream scoop, scoop out 10 -12 equal portions of batter and drop onto prepared baking sheet.

You can refrigerate for one hour, until firm, or you can dehydrate at 110 degrees for 8 hours.

For dehydrated version, try dipping into cacao chocolate.

~ Chapter 5 ~

SELF-LOVE

THERE ARE NEVER ENOUGH HOURS IN THE DAY.

There are never enough days in the week. No matter what you do, if you're like me, I bet you feel like you never have enough time to check everything off of your list...and that list keeps growing!

From the moment my eyes open I'm on the fast track all day long. Kids, homework, meal preparation, dogs, relationships, and oh yeah, did I mention my career? Often, it feels like I'm barely surviving.

What I've come to realize is that if I am not treating myself with love and attention, I have absolutely nothing to give back to those who rely on me and need me. If I'm overworked, exhausted and cranky, what kind of energy and message am I implanting in the brains of my children? I hope this chapter will remind you to treat yourself with the love and respect you would give to anyone else in your life.

The quality of our health and our lives is greatly affected by the many choices we make throughout our lifetimes.

We make choices every day about what we will put in our mouths, what we will purchase as a consumer, what activities we would like to participate in and with whom, and how to prioritize the tasks we want to accomplish.

One of the biggest decisions we can make is to improve the quality of our health and our lives by detoxification. When you hear the word "detoxification," you may immediately think about food. In this case, what I mean by detoxification is *to remove from our lives that which is no longer serving us.*

Our bodies are detoxifying every second. They have to in order to help us pay the price for the toxic overload in our environment. They are incredible machines. But they cannot cleanse efficiently without our help. Sure, we can try to steer away, the best we can, from pesticides, industrial wastes, synthetic medicine, food additives, car exhaust and cigarette smoke. Yes, we can try to eat organic, live foods, exercise and get more sleep.

We also need to examine what habits, patterns and relationships may be toxic in our lives.

Here are 10 ways to tell if your body is giving you a message that it needs to de-stress and detoxify:

1. Are you always in a hurry and find it difficult to sit still and relax?

2. Do you find yourself getting irritated?

3. Is your digestion not as optimal as you think it should be?

4. Do you have trouble falling asleep or wake up during the night?

5. Do you feel overworked or dislike your job?

6. Do you have a hard time accepting yourself just as you are?

7. Are you judgmental of yourself or others?

8. Do you feel a lack of purpose?

9. Do you hold onto your emotions and not share them?

10. Do you find it difficult to forgive others?

If we really want to detoxify, we need to let go of our negative emotional patterns so that we can experience the fullness of life physically, mentally and spiritually.

Here are 10 things to consider:

1. If your mind feels like the chatter won't stop, try meditation or sit quietly.

2. Balance work with play.

3. Spend time with people you love. Ditch those who don't support your vision.

4. Get deep, restful sleep.

5. Instead of holding grudges, find forgiveness.

6. Instead of expecting the worst, look for the best.

7. Try honesty and love instead of fear and doubt.

8. Instead of considering yourself unlucky or victimized, see each obstacle as an opportunity for transformation.

9. Instead of focusing on what you don't have, be grateful for all you do.

10. Instead of feeling like you always need to be in control, let go, surrender and watch the wealth of opportunity fall into your lap.

Why wait to receive an official medical diagnosis before you do something to improve your health? Why not start rejuvenating and purifying your body, mind and spirit now? It's the best health insurance you'll ever spend your money on.

I would imagine everyone experiences anxiety from time to time.

But have you ever had full blown panic attacks or had to go on antidepressants, because the symptoms were so bad your will wasn't strong enough to handle them? I have.

Yep, you heard me right. Upon graduating from college, I couldn't have foreseen the heightened levels of anxiety and pressure I'd undergo trying to become a successful lawyer. I was so afraid of letting my parents down and not achieving the level of stature and recognition I thought I needed in order to be seen, respected, or looked at with any measure of pride.

It was awful. I couldn't sleep. I couldn't concentrate. Any hope I had of holding a decent first-year associate job was going down the drain, and my emotional instability was the root of the disaster.

I couldn't eat. My weight got WAY too low. So low that most people diagnosed me with an eating disorder. Who knows...maybe I *did* have one. I needed control in my life, and I sure wasn't getting it anywhere else. My life had become a living hell, with me at its center.

I went to doctors to help ease my pain. I begged for anti-anxiety meds. What did I know at the time? Apparently nothing. Only that I needed to feel better. Not that I needed to get to the root of my problems.

So Xanax and Prozac became my friends. Yet I continued to push myself, still filled with the same fears, still doing the same old song and dance.

The meds just masked the truth of all these fears I was housing inside. The fear

of failure, disappointment, the pressure to succeed and be seen in a certain way. It was like I was carrying the weight of the world on my shoulders.

Anxiety is no joke. It is the worst feeling in the world to feel like your world is spinning out of control. And if you let external factors take over, you can let your life fall apart, masking the real issues.

Years later I turned to holistic healing. I knew there had to be a better solution than synthetic medications which I had learned were destroying my gut and not getting to the root of my problems.

I turned to yoga, self-awareness, changing my attitude and natural medicine.

It took me a while to become a believer. As a daughter of a physician, I thought going inward and using holistic products like essential oils was cuckoo. Where was the science?

Come on. Connecting to our true nature and using products from the earth were enough to heal? For real? YES!

Essential oils have been used for thousands of years to treat ailments, illnesses and emotional and hormonal imbalances.

Our sense of smell is connected to our limbic system, which is the seat of our emotions. Aromatherapy works at a cellular level to deal with all the emotional upheaval associated with anxiety. Essential oils can calm anxiety and even make it disappear before it arrives.

Here are 5 oils you can use to help calm your fears:

1. **Ylang Ylang,** pronounced (eeelang, eeelang), is notorious for balancing the solar and sacral plexus chakras, and can help alleviate stress and lower anxiety.

2. **Lavender** relieves mental stress and is a great relaxant. It can even help you sleep.

3. **Geranium** helps release negative memories and nervous tension. It is extraordinarily uplifting.

4. **Bergamot** is calming and uplifting. It is known for its antidepressant properties.

5. **Orange** is elevating for the mind and body and is known to bring joy and peace.

And these are just a few! The most effective way to use these oils is aromatically. Put a few drops in a diffuser and let the aroma take over. If you don't have a diffuser and need a quick release, put a drop or two in the palm of your hands and deeply inhale several times.

If you experience anxiety, try these great essential oils to combat it - you'll be surprised and amazed at the power of plants.

If you want to know where I get my oils, since you know I won't settle for anything but the best Certified Pure Therapeutic Grade, visit **www.mydoterra.com/hayleyhobson.**

It's Sunday and it should be a day off for most of us who work during the week.

I, of course, had to have my morning run which had me awake at the crack of dawn before my 3-year-old got up. When I got home, I had plenty to do. As you other moms know, the workday at home never stops.

After taking care of a few things online to prepare for the work week ahead, there were loads of laundry waiting, a house that needed to be cleaned, two dogs that were eager to get outside, and another 3-year-olds' birthday party to attend. Since my parents and in-laws were coming over for dinner, a stop at the market on the way home was warranted—having a few meals already prepared for the week would minimize after work or after school scrambling.

Sunday. Yeah! Sounds like a fun, relaxing day, doesn't it? I know I need lots of "quality" time with my daughter on the one day of the week that we should be enjoying our time together...

As I'm plodding along through this hectic day of relaxation and on the way home from the party, Madeline says, "Mommy! My throw-up is coming out!" Seriously? How does she even know what throw up is? Do I believe her? Is she being dramatic? Low and behold, the minute I pull into the Whole Foods parking lot, she regurgitated the juice box and popsicle (that I would never had fed her had it not been served to every other child at the party) all over. Ugh. The car seat is the worst.

What would you do? Yep, I took all her clothes off right there in the parking lot (thankfully it was 77 degrees out), dressed her in the only item of spare clothing I had in my car—a bathing suit one size too small—and marched right into the store. I hosed her down in the bathroom and proceeded to complete my grocery tour, hoping no one would notice my child in her ridiculous attire.

It's times like these I wish I were Superwoman. I wish I had magical powers to zoom through every mundane task that needs my attention, so I can be every version of the savvy self I want to be. I'd wish I had all the time in the world for my husband and daughter, and all the little things that fulfill me as an individual.

Some days there is barely enough time to scratch the surface and I can't seem to find the time to spend on the things I want to do the most. In an ideal world it would be phenomenal to do it all, have it all, and be it all. Superwoman can do it all and can move at the speed of light, fly from here to there, and pull off the stunts of a three-ring circus! Of course, the truth is I am NOT Superwoman...

Women are no longer just wives or mothers; our roles and interests have expanded beyond the home and into our own personal

aspirations. With more and more mothers out of the home and enjoying lives beyond parenting, I need to ask: how does one woman do everything and, if she can't do it all, what has to give?

Enormous pressure has been placed upon women who choose to be mothers and have careers. The truth is, children need their mamas and as much as I would like to be here and there, every waking second of every single day for my daughter, I can't be everything all the time.

Before I had my daughter I devoted my undivided attention to what I wanted to manifest personally in my life. I was top of my class in college. I practiced in a successful law firm. When I left the legal arena, I studied to be a Pilates instructor, yoga teacher and holistic health coach. I was running a successful business when my daughter was born. Did I have to give up my aspirations to become a mother? Was I going to have to choose, or apologize for having a brain and wanting more from my life than to be 'just' a mom? I wanted it all—like many women in this day.

"Having it all" is hard. I'd love to sit here and tell you that I'm always super duper mom, but I'm not. I'm a real woman who constantly has to juggle the demands of home life with my personal aspirations. It's really challenging to see my limitations. I can't do it all.

Back in the tribes, women had help. They recognized it and acknowledged it. Western Civilization outgrew its tribal roots, but we haven't evolved to have super-human powers to match our fast-paced minds. So, we must face reality. The ideas we hold about perfection: 'the perfect mom,' 'the perfect woman,' 'the perfect life,' are all illusions. When pitted against reality they're pipe dreams at best.

So can I really have it all? I still say yes. I don't believe that I can do it all by myself, nor should I try. I can still be a loving and attentive mom even if my energy and attention are divided. I don't have to be Superwoman to be a multifaceted human being—I just have to have a good game plan, beginning with what I value the most.

I believe that if you want to be the perfect mom in this age you may have to ask for help. Seriously, who can really handle the load that's been put upon us? Unless your weekends are relaxing walks in the park, you may need to assemble a team like I apparently need to do to help hold down the fort. Generations before us, women needed help.

It's OK that we do, too. Either that or something must go. Sacrifices must be made. Is it your yoga class one day? A sink full of dirty dishes? A few extra loads of laundry? Driving around in a car that really needs a bath (and now new seat belts)? Guess what? It's ok. You don't have to be perfect, but you can be perfectly happy. Let's see if we can get there together.

My day begins at 6:30am. I'm often on my laptop before I even brush my teeth.

Since I'm connecting with people all over the world on a daily basis, there are days I feel like I need to get online early because some of them have been up for hours.

I try to either get on my treadmill, or if the weather is warm enough, out the door for a run before my kids need to be shuffled off to school.

By 9am my day is in full swing and doesn't stop until I hit my pillow after 10pm.

Owning my own business, mentoring my team, raising two children and nurturing all the other relationships in my life can suck all the energy out of me if I let it. What do I desire most that I never have enough of? Time!

No matter how many hours there are in a day, it will never feel like enough. So prioritize your tasks daily, weekly, monthly and annually and then make sure you are nurturing yourself. If you are not taking the

I don't have to be Superwoman to be
a multifaceted human being.

best care of yourself, you cannot shine or be helpful to anyone else around you.

Here are a few tips that have helped me be that best version of myself:

1. **Spend a few minutes in the morning sipping.** I love my hot water with a few drops of lemon essential oil. It's my way of naturally helping my body detox. Maybe you prefer tea. Whatever your preference is, sit still for a few minutes and let the morning sink in.

2. **Schedule in your exercise.** If I don't exercise early, I've found that it may never happen at all. I've learned that lesson all too many times as I'm staring at my computer at 3pm—still in my pajamas!

3. **Eat foods that nourish you and give you energy.** After my run, I juice my own fruits and vegetables. The live enzymes from the juice go directly into my bloodstream and set me up for feeling alive the rest of the day. I also make sure my refrigerator is stocked with fresh produce all the time so I can easily prepare a healthy, vegan meal or snack without resorting to junk or processed foods.

4. **Stop and breathe.** There are definitely moments in every day when I feel completely overwhelmed. I'm sure you do too.

So stop. Pause. Put things in perspective. Prioritize. Breathe. Let go.

Notice how your mood can shift when you give yourself a little space.

5. **Do something nice for yourself every day.** Maybe this means wearing your favorite pair of jeans or yoga pants, getting a massage, a pedicure, putting on makeup, or on those days where you are in lock down in front of the computer, just taking a shower and washing your hair! It's okay to indulge yourself.

6. **Learn to rest when you are tired.** Our bodies are very intelligent and they are in communication with us all the time. If you are not in tune with your body it is going to be harder for you to figure out what it is trying to say to you. Pay attention to the messages you are getting and take a break or even a nap when needed.

7. **Say NO if you need to.** This is a piece of advice I need to listen to more myself. As a mom, a wife, a daughter and a mentor to dozens of coaches on my team, I feel like I am always "doing" for others. It's okay to say no when we don't have the time or simply don't feel like it. You don't have to be superwoman and please everyone.

8. **Appreciate what is around you.** No matter what is going on in your life, you are blessed in so many ways. You are breathing fresh air, have food on your plate and have someone in your life that loves you and cares about you (even if it's your pet.) Yes, there are days or even months when your life doesn't look like the fairy tale you want it to be. The secret is to have gratitude for the big picture. Somewhere in every tragedy is a lesson we can share and I promise you that even the worst situation can turn out to be our biggest blessing.

9. **Send some love to someone else.** I find I get easily caught up in what feels like endless chores and work...don't you? Our world is intense. Even on days when I think I'll get a break, hundreds of emails flood my inbox, or my 3-year-old gets sick. No matter how busy I get, I try to remind myself to send some love to someone else. Maybe it's a tap on the shoulder, a hug or simply a phone call. As human beings, we thrive on love—so don't be selfish with it. Reach out and let someone important in your life know how much they mean to you.

10. **Give yourself a pat on the back.** I know it is so easy to get down on yourself. We all do. There is always something on my to-do list that I did not have time to get done. There are plenty of conversations and situations I wish I had handled differently. We need to remember everything we have accomplished. Don't be your hardest critic. Give yourself a little more love too!

Try these steps out for yourself. The key is to learn the tricks and trades that work for you and that will keep you strong, nourished and constantly evolving.

I used to be a Bitch.

It was 2002. I was living in the City of Angels, trying to make it on my own. My first stab at a career had ended. Five years in the practice of law was all I could take. I tried... Believe me, I tried.

I started as a corporate Bankruptcy attorney for Carolco Pictures—do you remember them? They produced the *Terminator* and many more. After two years of reorganizing, I found myself intrigued with the world of Entertainment. It's funny—most people relocate to Los Angeles to be involved in that world. I had been there for 7 years already and it had taken me that long to bite. I'm glad I did. It taught me a great lesson that I'm still in the process of implementing.

I took a job at Jersey Films. Not a good move, or so I thought at the time. Here I had been thinking I was "moving up" on the career ladder and instead, I became a glorified assistant to an assistant.

The job sucked, AND I had taken a not-so-small pay cut for it. Played the cards, lost the hand. I moved on.

Next, I landed at E-Entertainment. This job may actually have been worse. Silly me. I thought I had been hired as a L-A-W-Y-E-R who graduated cum laude from a prestigious school. I guess not. I found myself doing the same grunt work I had been doing 12 years earlier without a college degree or any prior work experience.

The mentality in Hollywood is that people are dying to be a part of its glamorous world and will basically work for minimum wage no matter how qualified they are.

Not me. I was miserable. Resentful. Self-serving. I thought I deserved better. I was smart, educated and reliable. So why did I feel like a bottom sucking, worthless piece of sh*t? To top it all off, not surprisingly, my first marriage was falling apart.

We always have a choice. We can either tune in to the universe and accept the gifts it offers to us—no matter how disguised they may seem at the time—or we can fight and lose the battle. I had no idea the universe had my back at the time so I fought it every step of the way.

I was a TOTAL BITCH!

Not on purpose, of course. I really had no idea how poorly I was behaving...but everyone else around me did. No one liked me besides my family and my closest friends. Honestly, I wonder now if they really liked me at the time, or were just putting up with me because they thought they had to.

So now here I was with no job at all, no husband, living in this crazy, intense city where everyone was out for himself, biting to survive.

At some point, I stopped sleeping. Well, not completely. I'd go to bed every night around 10pm and without fail, I was up at 1am. It actually became a game I had with myself. I'd open my eyes, guess the time was 1:03am or 1:07am, look at the clock and smile that I could be that on track. I'd be up until 4:00 am, fall back asleep for an hour or two and then my blaring alarm would jolt me up again. Perfect. Exhausted and bitchy... What a great combination to start the day.

At some point I scheduled an appointment with my doctor so I could beg for something to keep me asleep at night. He knew me quite well. I had been there several times over the past few years with various maladies. You name it. Sinus infections, IBS symptoms, the flu. If it came around, I got it. It's no wonder. My body was a mess. Undernourished in every sense of the word. Overstimulated. Completely stressed out.

Not that there is really any excuse to act like a self-deserving, self-centered, thoughtless bitch, but when your body is not getting the nourishment it needs, how can you possibly give back positive, loving light?

I'd sit in that waiting room, staring at my watch, wondering how anyone could have the audacity to keep me waiting so long. Didn't he know I had places to go and people to see too? My time was just as important as his. I made that perfectly clear to the assistant behind the desk.

Finally, I was seen and walked out with what I needed! I was looking forward to sleeping through the night! But I was in for a surprise... It was more than the night I slept through. I couldn't drag myself out of bed after 14 or 15 hours. My body was limp...I had no energy. No life. No personality. Not even my bitchy one. I was sucked dry.

I thought I'd adjust to the medication but it continued for weeks. My life wasn't getting better. It was getting worse. I was falling into emptiness.

I called up my doctor and asked him what he had given me. I told him I could not function. You know what I found out? He had given me medication for a schizophrenic. He thought I had a personality disorder!

Yes, I was unhappy. Yes, I was a bitch. But...the only personality disorder I had was that I had not yet tapped into my inner self. I could not feel my heart. I was not being nourished by the "primary foods" in my life that included so much more than I was actually putting in my mouth.

I needed love.
I needed guidance.
I needed support.
I needed compassion.
I needed a nurturing relationship.
I needed a career I loved.

Once I realized that, I took
the steps I needed to make it
all happen.

I needed love. I needed guidance. I needed support. I needed compassion. I needed a nurturing relationship. I needed a career I loved.

Once I realized that, I took the steps I needed to make it all happen.

It's taken me years to walk along the path I've been heading, and I'm not saying I'm perfect. God knows I'm far from perfect.

Now, I am finally able to look at my destiny differently. I will never again be "stuck" in a life I don't want to be living. Now I have a right to be happy. I am allowed to write the fairytale I want my life to look like. It's up to me to create it. No one is going to make my dreams come true, other than myself. I know that if I send positive light out into the universe it will come back to me tenfold.

Best of all, when I lay my head down on my pillow, I actually sleep through the night.

Staying motivated all year long... even though your New Years resolutions are long gone.

Do you dread January 1st? You need to get your butt back in shape, but you also know it can be so difficult to stay motivated once you start.

The gyms are packed once the New Year rolls around, as people desperately try to achieve their resolutions to shed a few extra unwanted pounds, get fit, or both. It can be nearly impossible just to find parking at your local club or studio! You may even have to wait in line just to hop on a treadmill or place your mat down in the hallway. In a few weeks, though, the parking spots reappear and whatever location you have chosen to frequent is not so crowded anymore. What has happened? Why do people fail to stay motivated?

So many people are making New Years resolutions but within weeks they are back to their old patterns. This does not have to be you this year! I've got a few guidelines that will really help you achieve your goals.

Dream Big

When we manifest energy, the universe conspires with us to make it happen. You cannot dream big enough. Visualize what you want to look like, feel like or what pace 10k you want to run and write it down in your journal. You can even pin a photo of your ideal body, a specific yoga pose you want to get into, or what your running stride looks like up on your bathroom mirror or on your computer screen. Just place it somewhere where you can look at it every day for motivation.

Make A Promise To Yourself

I often get in the habit lately of eating snacks very late at night. When I do so, my sleep suffers, I wake up a little groggier in the morning and my belly feels bloated. I want to break this habit. This may mean I have to eat more nutritionally dense food during the day. So my promise to myself is that when I wake up, I will make myself eat within 2 hours and not wait until 11am! Another promise to myself is that I will make time for a proper lunch rather than eating on the go. I know that when I get adequate food in during the day with all of the phytonutrients my body needs, I will not crave snacks late at night.

Be Specific With Your Promise

Your "plan" may be to eat healthier this year. What does that really mean? Are you going to cut processed food out of your diet? Stop eating after 7pm like me? Add more greens to your plate? Resolve to bring your own lunches to work each day? You've got to be specific. You may have the best intentions but if you are not providing yourself with a road map, you'll have no way to measure your progress.

Set A Consequence For Yourself If You Don't Live Up To Your Promise

One of the things I have been doing for myself lately is setting a consequence for myself if I don't live up to my promise. For instance, I love to watch certain shows on TV like Grey's Anatomy, Scandal and Revenge. I record them every week on my DVR. I have decided that as a consequence to me eating late at night, I am going to delete my shows so I cannot watch them! Agh! I don't want that to happen! So y ou know what? You can be darn sure I am going to finish eating for the day by 7pm!

Remember that to achieve your goals, you must have a plan of action—and if that plan has not worked in the past, change your plan. Do something different. For example, if your plan last year was to lose a few pounds and you took up running to get there but hated running, change your plan. Go to a spin class. Get in the pool. Assess your diet—the foods that you're eating, how your food is prepared, what you are doing while you are eating and the time of day you sit down to eat. With a different plan, you may have different results.

Remember, this is your life and you get to design it!

You are the author and you get the write the story exactly how you'd like it to be laid out.

Are you going to write a story you love this year?

My three year old daughter, Madeline, and I have an evening routine.

Every night after dinner, we head upstairs and take a bath in our master bathroom. In fact, I don't think Madeline has ever been in her own bathtub!

Taking a bath together is our way of winding down at night and spending a few moments together, close and personal.

There are so many benefits to taking a bubble bath.

First, a bubble bath allows you to focus on you. You get to draw your attention to your inner sense of self. Your entire day may have to be spent caring for other people or being engaged with work—or at least mine is! So soaking in the tub allows me the time to reflect and clear my mind of endless details called life. Now I know I mentioned that I am not alone in the tub, but I use this time to reflect and focus on my little sweetheart since during the work day, I don't get the opportunity to spend as much time with her as I'd like. We use a shower gel I found with botanical extracts in our bath that have a fresh tangerine fragrance. Smells delish! Sometimes I add relaxing essential oils to my bath salts. Extra bonus!

Second, a bubble bath is the perfect environment for you to relax. The warm water, bubbles and your favorite scent create a recipe for calmness and serenity. Some of my favorites are Lavender, Bergamot, Roman Chamomile and Ylang Ylang. After the water begins to move, the scents of the oils rise with the steam of the water. You can lay back and enjoy the amazing benefits of aromatherapy.

Finally, a bubble bath can really improve the condition of your skin. A soak in the tub leaves you with smoother, silkier skin. The water softens your skin thus creating an easier surface for exfoliation. Try a loofah or pumice stone on rougher patches of your skin after a bath and feel how your skin softens to the touch!

For the past few weeks, I had been planning on attending a yoga event in South Denver.

One of my favorite yoga teachers and mentors, Desiree Rumbaugh, was coming to town. There was no way I was going to miss seeing her.

I live in North Boulder, so South Denver is a drive for me. I pulled up the directions on Mapquest as I was running out the door. According to my reliable source, the studio was forty-five minutes away. I looked at the time. 12:30 p.m. The event was not until 1:30 p.m. One hour. Perfect. I had plenty of time.

As I got on the road, I realized only the first page of the directions had printed out. Great. I knew how to get out of my neighborhood and head into Denver. What I really needed was the second page.

I need to clarify this scenario for a second so you understand what goes on inside of my head when I get behind the wheel. Let's just say it's not good. I DO NOT do well with directions. Not sure what that's about, but I'm actually going to admit that I'd rather hop a flight to New York and negotiate myself around the city than get on a highway and try to figure out where I'm going in a town I call home.

So here I am on US 36, driving seventy miles an hour, without a clue. Do I hop on I-25?

I-70? I had tried calling the studio and even emailed them before I left just to confirm I knew where I was going, but they were not picking up.

I was in the middle of living one of my biggest nightmares.

The forty-five minute drive turned into an hour and a half. It was WAY farther than I had anticipated. I was already thirty minutes late. And judging by the traffic at 1:00 p.m., I had no friggin' idea how I'd get home any earlier at 4:00 p.m. during rush hour to pick up my little one from pre-school on time.

I turned around and went home.

SO pissed at myself. I started beating myself down.

Why didn't I call the studio yesterday? Why didn't I review the directions with my husband? He's my navigation tool when I'm in a pinch. Why didn't I look at the directions before I left the house? Why didn't I give myself more driving time?

Damn. I couldn't let it go. I was on the verge of tears.

This was my entire day. Sitting on my butt in friggin' traffic driving around like a crazy person...

And the only person I could be pissed off at was myself.

I made a mistake. I had not prepared myself well enough.

Check this out. Every single person on this planet makes mistakes. We are here to learn, and mistakes are just part of our process.

I will lay cash down on the fact that so many of you beat yourself up over something silly like I did yesterday.

Here's the deal. Who cares if I missed the event? I'll catch Desiree this summer at the Wanderlust Festival in Copper Mountain and at the Omega Institute in Rhineback, NY. And so what if I sat in the car all afternoon? I actually enjoyed being able to catch up, live in the flesh, with several of my associates in Connecticut, Chicago, NY, and Houston that I normally am only able to communicate with via email or text message.

What I've come to learn is that character is not defined by the mistakes we make. Character is what we do in the face of adversity.

The lesson I learned that day was to prepare the night before I go anywhere. And when I can learn from my mistakes and you can learn from yours, we will not repeat them, right? Our mistakes will help us evolve and grow. That, my friend, is the basis of life.

Neil Gaiman, award-winning author, couldn't have said it better, "If you're making mistakes, it means you're out there doing something."

Our mistakes show our humanity and humility.

What mistakes have you made recently? And what have you learned from that incident?

My husband and I actually went out on a date last week.

It feels like it never happens anymore. Two kids at home. Don't feel like paying a babysitter. Both of us crazy busy with what we like to call LIFE.

So, the babysitter comes, we get in the car and can't decide where to go. We start rattling off the usuals, boring ourselves to tears.

Finally, call us crazy, we agreed to try someplace we'd never been. Totally out of our comfort zone. A menu we'd never seen. Now, I know that may not be a big deal to you, but as a gluten-free, 90% raw vegan, that's a BIG deal to me. As you can imagine, most restaurants do not cater to my kind, and it can become quite stressful going out.

But you know what? The restaurant was delightful; the chef made me feel like a superstar, and I even learned how to spice up my coconut kale recipe.

I tell you this story because on our way out, we felt stuck. On our way out, we felt bored. It even entailed massive energy just to get out of the house.

Do you ever have those days where you feel like you're doing the same old, same old? Mondays always feel like Mondays. Weekends don't even feel like weekends anymore. You go to bed at eleven. You wake up at 6:30. Your workout stays the same. You're going through the motions. No variety in your meals. Grocery list never changes. Vacation destinations, if they even exist, never vary. Hanging out in the same old circles...

Now, I don't mean to discredit feeling comfy in your shoes. Security blankets are always nice, but we can get stuck in much larger areas of our lives. If we don't try something new every once in a while to get out of the funk we're in, our moods, levels of anxiety, and overall health will be deeply affected long term.

I hear many people, especially women, talk a lot about feeling stuck. They *thought* they knew what they wanted, but they soon realize they don't. Their eyes *were* on their prize, but suddenly, their path is no longer clear.

Are you one of them? Are you still struggling with what you really want? Are you grasping at straws? Do you feel stuck more so than not?

In order to become unglued from the past, you MUST be willing to try something new. Often times, when our lives or relationships aren't working, it's because we are doing the same old sh*t that is no longer working for us... And maybe it really never was.

If you're craving a change, you must make a change. Maybe it's as simple as trying a new restaurant. Or maybe it's bolder, like trying a new career path. Are you ready to figure out what change you need to make?

Well, here you go. I've got a few tips you can try to get unstuck.

You're going to have to go in and be real with yourself. Grab a journal and make sure you take the time and are not distracted by media, relationships, work, or kids. This is time just for you.

1. Identify where you are stuck.

2. What does stuck feel like in your body? Where does the feeling originate? Describe what you feel in detail.

3. What do you want or wish to be different?

4. What would it take to get there? Do you have to be honest with yourself or maybe someone else?

5. Write down all your fears.

Once you have complied this list, begin to focus on the solution. By journaling, you will have identified the problem, so the solution is the logical next step.

The hardest part is often trying something different. However, if you want a different outcome, you MUST make different choices.

If having a painful conversation with someone (including yourself) frightens you, good! Face your fear! Get beyond it so you can move forward.

If you don't, you'll inevitably suffer later.

You are in charge of your own reality.

Seriously. You are. If something is no longer serving you, LET IT GO. If you need to make a shift, do it.

Don't wait until you are suffering. You will snap. Act now, and along the way, be very gentle with yourself.

Have faith and trust in yourself and your capabilities in the moment. You may be able to do more tomorrow than you can today, and that is OK. Have patience.

Chapter 5
YOGA SEQUENCE

1.   SAVASANA
2.   ARDHA APANASANA
3.   SUPTA PADANGHUSTASANA
4.   APANASANA
5.   SUKASANA
6.   SUKASANA - UTTHITA HASTA ARMS
7.   SUKASANA - ARMS REACHING FORWARD
8.   BIDALASANA
9.   ADHA MUKHA VIRASANA
10.   ADHO MUKHA SVANASANA
11.   UTTANASANA
12.   ADHO MUKHA SVANASANA
13.   HALF SUN SALUTE - (REPEAT 3X)
14.   VIRABHADRASANA 1
15.   VIRABHADRASANA 2
16.   TRIKONASA
17.   ARDHA CHANDRASANA
18.   TRIKONASA
19.   EKA PADA RAJAKAPOTASANA
20.   JANU SIRSASANA
21.   BADDHA KONASANA
22.   UPAVISTA KONASANA
23.   PASCHIMOTANASANA
24.   HALASANA
25.   SALAMBHA SARVANGASANA
26.   HALASANA
27.   KARNIPADASANA
28.   MATSYASANA
29.   SAVASANA

FORWARD FOLDS

HALF SUN
SALUTE

(REPEAT 3X)
SEE PAGE 12

Visit **http://bit.ly/12Vw3PI**
to access Hayley's downloadable
Yoga class, *Happy Hips*.

Raw, Beanless Hummus

Ingredients

- 2-3 organic zucchinis, chopped
- 3/4 raw tahini
- Juice from 2 lemons
- 2 tsp Himalayan Sea Salt
- 3-4 garlic cloves
- Splash of Braggs Amino Acids
- 1 drop Lemon essential oil

Instructions

Whisk or blend all ingredients until creamy.

> "One should eat to live, not live to eat."
> ~MOLIERE

Vegan Lo-Mein

Ingredients

For the low-mein
- 1 package of rice noodles
- 1-2 carrots, sliced
- 1/2 yellow onion, sliced thin
- 1 cup baby bella mushrooms, sliced
- 1 cup sprouted mung beans
- 2 large leaves of swiss chard, cut into strips
- 1 tbsp extra virgin olive oil
- green onion for garnish
- additional options: chopped green cabbage, water chestnuts, bamboo shoots

For the sauce
- 1 tbsp freshly grated ginger
- 2 cloves garlic
- 1 tbsp agave nectar
- 1/4 cup wheat-free tamari or Braggs Amino Acids
- 1/4 cup vegetable broth
- 2 tbsp orange juice
- 1 tsp sesame oil
- 1 drop Ginger essential oil
- 1 drop Orange essential oil

Instructions

Wash, chop and prep your veggies. Add extra virgin olive oil to a large skillet or wok on medium/high heat. Add veggies and lightly stir-fry for about 5 minutes. Add swiss chard halfway through (this only needs a minute or two.) Cook noodles in another boiling pot until soft. Combine all sauce ingredients in a small stovetop pan and cook on low/medium heat. When sauce has thickened, combine sauteed veggies, noodles and sauce in a large wok and stir-fry for an additional 5 minutes.

Chapter 6

Business & Prosperity

HAVE YOU EVER FELT LIKE THERE WAS A TIME IN YOUR LIFE WHEN YOU COULDN'T ACTUALLY MAKE YOUR OWN CHOICES?

I did. The influence of others, primarily my parents, with their hopes and expectations of me, spoke much louder than my own feelings and desires.

By the time I showed up in my college dormitory room, I felt lost. I realized I hadn't even chosen the school I wanted to go to. When applying to college, the list had become my parents' list and in the end I chose what they expected of me.

A respectable profession to my parents upon graduation meant medicine or law so off to law school I went. As the perfect overachiever, I persevered those grueling years and landed a coveted first year associate position in a very prestigious law practice. Sadly, I came to realize that who I had become did not reflect my truest desires.

I was living a life others had planned for me and I was uninspired, unfulfilled, and craving something more—something ME.

I wanted to live a life I loved, to make my passions my career, and to make choices that reflected my values and my heart.

The problem was, I didn't trust myself. I had become so programmed to do and become someone I was not, I really had to take a step back and look deep inside of myself. I was scared. I was going to have to walk away from everything I had worked for and the person I had become in order to be who I really wanted to be. I had to be strong and courageous.

Last week I started packing for my week-long yoga retreat.

Yoga clothes? A necessity. Yoga mat? I like to travel with a light one. Journal? Of course. Make-up? Leaving that at home this trip. Laptop? Ugh. I can't seem to leave that one at home.

Technology has allowed all of us to have a lot more flexibility in our work lives these days but at what expense? Can we ever really unplug? I am still trying to figure out how. Every time I pack to go anywhere, I bring my laptop, charger, iPad, charger, iPhone, charger, batter extender, Blue tooth earpiece, charger, MiFi wireless network device, and charger. I look like I own an electronics store.

I try to chalk it up to the fact that I'm in my 40's and these are my income generating years. I recently left a job in management to work full time on my holistic coaching and business mentoring business, so I had to revamp my website and get the word out to everyone about the three nutrition programs I just wrote, my exploding essential oil business and everything else I've been up to. You know what that means. Yes, I've been living on social media, blogging and guest blogging like crazy, writing newsletters and giving educational workshops all over the country. I need to keep on top of my game in this crazy, competitive economy.

I'm always questioning the price my body is paying for being such a work-a-holic. Isn't the point of this yoga retreat to relax and recharge? Don't I deserve a break after so many months of 12-hour days? So why is my laptop open?!! Do I really need to be scheduling my posts for the entire week on Facebook right now when I feel that warm summer breeze coming in through my window? NO! I'm on VACATION!

I'm pretty sure I'm not the only one who finds myself sneaking onto my laptop or glancing a peek at my iPhone in order to squeeze just a bit more work in. There are always those few minutes before bed, the few minutes in the morning, the few minutes relaxing on the beach, the few minutes while the kids are playing games… The list begins to expand until we begin to realize that we are simply doing what we do at home but in a slightly more pleasant location.

Isn't the point of getting away, especially on family vacations, to spend more time with ourselves and with those we love? Life is so busy at home I often feel like I am not spending any time with those who sleep under the same roof as me. So something just isn't right when you and your family plan a vacation to get rid of the intensity of life and then you bring your work with you!

So here I was at Kripalu, one of the most world-renowned yoga & meditation retreats. I practiced 5 hours a day with one of my favorite teachers, Desiree Rumbaugh, who always has a way of bringing me back into the reality of who I really am. I head back to my room, feeling light and refreshed, with a natural smile on my face. I see my laptop staring me at me from the corner of my eye... Ignore it! Ignore it! I reach for the book by the side of my bed. Then I hear my iphone beeping. Oh god, come on! Hmmm… well there are a few things I could take care of. All of a sudden, what I told myself would take 15 minutes sucked me in for 3 hours!

Why don't I get it? Why don't any of us get it? Going on a vacation meant taking a break! Many of us Americans are obsessed with working all the time, no breaks, no stopping—even when it comes to family! Everyone, myself (especially) included, needs to just stop and take a pause with no exceptions.

Next vacation I am determined not to repeat this year's mistakes. So here are some of my new tips for actually leaving work behind.

1. Set auto-reply 'away' messages for your email accounts.

2. If you manage other people, delegate tasks that you would normally do.

3. Trust other people to do the work—you don't have to do everything!

4. Let everyone know you're going on vacation ahead of time so they can schedule around your time off, not bother you, and make things work without you.

You may be a very important person, but the work world will keep revolving even if you disappear for a week or two! Put away your phone and computer because no matter what happens, it will tempt you to just take that one call or answer that one email. It's not worth it. Remember your priorities. I know how hard it is in this technologically modern era to just let go of the mobile world, but the memories of your vacation will last forever. Those emails will *most certainly* not.

Do you wish you were spending more time doing things you absolutely love?

You know those things that jazz you up and cause your heart to beat faster? Do you wish the passion you have for your hobbies could actually be your business and career? Then, as icing on the cake, make money doing something you love?

If you already have your kick ass job, or are not planning on starting your own business, this may not be for you. I'm writing this for those of you who feel stuck like I did, but knew there must be another way. Surprise! You're right! There is definitely a way to make money doing something you love to do every day! People often ask me:

- Why did you decide to start an online business?

- How did you set your own schedule/hours and work from home?

- How did you get so many people following you on Facebook in such a short time?

- How do you come up with such great content for your Facebook page and in your newsletters?

- How did you put all of your websites together?

- How do you market your business without sounding sales-ey?

- How are you managing to run your own business and raise a family?

- How are you getting to do something you love every day?

As you have learned by now from my stories in this book, I worked for several years in corporate America as an attorney. I knew after a short while that I was not going to be able to sit at a desk all day long writing combative argumentative briefs and making someone else tons of money.

I had a passion for fitness and wellness and so I began to write the next chapter of my life. I studied and trained to become a Pilates and yoga teacher and a certified holistic health coach. Yay for me! Right? Well, not really... Although I was now in a field that was driving my passions daily, let's face it, the money was not great. I was working crazy hours and it was not paying off. And, most importantly, if I did not work, I did not get paid. Not good!

For years, I was SO frustrated. I was working my butt off. My schedule was never really my own. I was really at the whim of my clients' schedules. I felt guilty if I took a day off. I got pissed off if I got sick. I was getting burned out.

So, knowing there had to be a better way, I hired a life coach and began to design my dreams. That project, in itself, was a crazy experiment. I had no idea what I really wanted until I started writing it down!

In addition, I started doing some research and began to follow other women out there in cyberspace who had thousands of subscribers and who I knew were doing something right. Finally, I found a group of smart, motivated, entrepreneurial women, like me, with whom I could bounce ideas off of.

The first few months were scary and hard. I took a risk and quit my "day job." Luckily I had some money saved up and my husband was still working. We did have to watch our wallets for awhile. However, I knew that in order to make my new life manifest itself before my eyes, I was going to have to go all in.

It was also evident that to make my online business work, I had to be seen. I hired someone to design a beautiful website for me and as my business began to take off, that one website actually turned into 4! I'm sure you've heard the motto—to make money, you will have to spend some money first. Knowing it was an investment in my life, I jumped in without hesitation. For me, there was no other choice. Right away I started to see amazing changes in my career and my online presence!

I spent about six months working my butt off and implementing all I had been learning. Let's face it, any new business takes a major time commitment in the beginning. I very quickly went from feeling overworked, stressed out, burned out, miserable and confused, to loving my life AND making money!

When I went back and reviewed the dreams I had written six months prior, they had all come true. When you send that kind of intention into the universe, it does come back to you. I promise.

So why am I telling you all of this? It's definitely not to brag or make you jealous. I'm telling you my story because I know you, too, can be happy doing something you love. I'm telling you my story to inspire you to define your dreams and to help you figure out a way to make money living a life you love.

I know that you, too, can:

- Turn your dreams into a profitable career.

- Be clear and concise about your business goals.

- Build your ideal website with the most amazing content.

- Attract your ideal clients.

- Get tons of subscribers to your blog or newsletter.

- Turn your subscribers into paying customers.

- Sell your services and products that you know are helping your clients without sounding sales-ey.

- Rock your world!

You've only got one life.

What are you going to start doing with it?

When are you going to start?

Gratitude for the Big Picture.

A few weeks ago, I received an upsetting phone call from one of the yoga studios for whom I had been teaching a few classes. My classes were being cut. I was stunned, hurt, angry and immediately began to question myself. Did the students not like me? Was I not a good teacher? Were people complaining? It's so easy to go to that negative place where insecurity, self-doubt and self-criticism start creeping in.

My head began to spin. Only a few months ago, I had just given up 8 classes a week to work on other aspects of my business. Having two more classes cut left me only teaching one! How could this be? What had I done wrong? I thought my classes had been doing well. I should never have given up those other classes. I was barely teaching in the community anymore, something I had loved doing for the past 15 years. I was devastated.

After taking a couple of days to better assess the situation, I was able to cool down. I realized the decision was not a reflection on my teaching at all. My clients loved my classes. In fact, when they heard the news, they all started contacting me to see what they could do to bring me back.

The truth was that the owner of the studio and I didn't see eye-to-eye. I had known this for a very long time. I had different visions for the studio and for myself that didn't align with her vision and you know what? That was ok.

In the heat of the moment, it is always easy to feel like your world is spiraling down. That is what happened to me upon hearing the news. I cherished the few classes I taught each week; I loved the precious hours I spent moving my clients through asanas, teaching them to breathe and let go, and witnessing their progress. Yoga has been a major part of my life for the past twenty years, and I love sharing my passion for my practice with others. So when someone else makes a decision for me that I was not prepared for, my emotions took control.

After reflecting upon the situation, I recognized there were other studios where I could share my passion. I would be able to pick up more classes at a different location sometime in the future. It really wasn't the end of the world. I thought about all that I have to be grateful for. Even if the glass looked half full, I was thankful that there was a glass with something in it at all!

I have had an unbelievable year. I've launched a new business that I love running and is turning out to be extremely successful. I hosted my second YogaWorks teacher training with 20 graduates. I have my health and in fact, I feel better than ever before. I have two beautiful daughters who I adore watching grow up each day.

I have a wonderful, caring husband who supports me in all of my endeavors. It can be easy to feel unfortunate, but when I look at the bigger picture, I have so much to celebrate.

You may not be completely satisfied with some aspects of your life. Perhaps you're unhappy at your job, or you're in a relationship that is no longer serving you.

Always remember you are the author of your life.

You get to decide what you want to change that will bring you more in alignment with your true self. As you grab the reins and take control, celebrate the joy that is present in your life now. Look at the bigger picture. I'm sure you will find plenty for which to be thankful.

My REAL education in business came AFTER my law degree—when I joined MARIE FORLEO'S B-SCHOOL online business program. Marie's program taught me how to build a business and life I love.

If you are interested in building your business, contact me at www.hayleyhobson.com and I'll share even more!

MARIE'S PRODUCT GUIDE:
https://s3.amazonaws.com/bschool/
BSchoolProductTour2013.pdf   OR

MARIE'S REGISTRATION PAGE:
http://rhhbschool.com

Be sure to tell them I sent you!

Integrating our passions with our career should come easy. We should have a right to do what we love.

For so many of us, it is more difficult than you'd imagine. So many people have an experience like I did. We literally don't realize we have the right to choose.

For others, "success" has arrived, and we think that's what matters most. Even if these "successful" people feel unfulfilled and unhappy, the thought of walking away and starting over is unfathomable. Isn't success supposed to be the 'end game?'

Not when your heart isn't in it.

What would happen if you were taught to make choices that affect your LIFE with your heart instead of your head?

What would happen if you started to visualize your dreams and could see them in front of you?

You'd be surprised.

The universe conspires in your favor when you are true to your heart and when you are honest about what you desire.

Do you feel like you need to make a change in your career, a relationship, your family, your body, your diet, your health or your spirituality?

If you had to rate these areas of your life on a scale of 1-10 where would they rank?

If they are not at a 10, why not? You deserve to live the most amazing life you can live.

You should be determined to help yourself grow and succeed.

It's time to …

- Get healthy.

- Find inspiration and support.

- Get out of a career if it does not align with your vision.

- Move beyond your self-limiting beliefs.

- Make a change in your life that reflects the core of your heart.

- Hold yourself accountable to people you can trust.

- Get in touch with your true desires.

- Live your life with vitality, passion and purpose.

- Live a life you LOVE.

You are ready for abundance.

This is your life.

Do you need to make a change?

And if so, are you ready?

In 1994 I graduated at the top of my class from Rutgers School of Law. A path I had chosen. Or so I thought.

Let's face it. Do we really know at 20 years old what we want to do the rest of our lives? Many people don't know the answer to that question in their 40s!

After five years of living in the rat race, I flat out quit. That's right. I quit.

And I'm not afraid to say it: all of those years, all of that education, and all of that money went down the drain. Wasted. Or so my parents thought.

When they heard what I wanted to do instead, I thought they'd have a heart attack. Yoga teacher? Pilates instructor? OMG. "You'll never make a living," they gasped.

Maybe not. But at least I'd be living my life with passion and grace. Following my dreams. Listening to my heart.

So off I went, and you know what? I did make a living, and it wasn't such a bad one. I had my own little studio. I hired a small staff of instructors; my schedule was always booked. My classes were always packed, and eventually I was asked to manage a very large Mind and Body Department at a very respectable Health Club. Maybe it was the law degree.

But after 15 years, I was exhausted. Although I loved helping others heal themselves from pain, inflammation, stress, and chronic tightness (not to mention my staff of over 30 I often felt the need to micromanage), I knew I needed another change.

I wasn't really a business owner. I was an employee of a very large corporation, making someone else money and acting as a sole proprietor on the side.

If I didn't work, I didn't get paid. So I always worked.

I knew I needed to support my health. I knew I needed more freedom. And by this I mean freedom with time and with my finances. I stepped down from my management position. I gave up almost all of my private clients. I stopped teaching classes.

I was going into debt. I had no idea how I'd pay my bills. But I knew that in order to launch a new avenue of my business that would give me more financial freedom in the long run, I had to let go of what was no longer serving me. I had to let go of what was holding me back from soaring full steam ahead.

I went back to school and became a Board Certified Health Coach. I did an intensive eight-week online business school. I spent months teaching myself everything I needed to know in order to turn myself into a social media guru.

I was going to take my business online. I was going to incorporate a product line. I was going to start making residual income.

Imagine this:

I was going to make money whether I was working or not.

I'd have the freedom to travel.

I could spend time with my kids.

I could work from wherever I wanted.

I'd no longer be tied down to anyone else's schedule but my own.

It's not easy starting a new business. But what I've found is that when you do make the time, when you're dedicated, when you really want to make something work, it will.

And so six months in, I was offered an amazing opportunity to take my business national. It was an opportunity I couldn't pass up. It would involve a lot of travel. I'd be on the road more often than I'd be home with my family.

When I approached the subject with my husband, he wasn't keen on being a single parent for four months but after numerous discussions, we ultimately decided, as a team, that the travel would be a wise investment in our future. And we'd limit it to four months.

As part of our "agreement" I committed to getting on a plane once a week to meet all the associates who were already working with me and help them grow their businesses, which would ultimately help me grow mine.

When the four months were up, we decided the travel should continue once a month going forward in order to continue to build the business.

Traveling isn't easy.

When I wake up in the morning, I often don't know what day of the week it is. Or what time zone I'm in. My body is constantly in a state of flux. The beds I'm sleeping in aren't always ideal. The food I'm eating is sometimes questionable. I'm not getting the exercise I'm used to.

But you know what? It's been 5-6 months. Even after the first two months, I saw my numbers double. It's an investment we're making in tomorrow, so that we can work less and live our passions.

Finally, ask yourself these questions and get your process started.

Do you feel like you need to make a change but something's still stopping you?

What are you afraid of giving up?

What obstacles are in your way?

What excuses are you still giving?

Hayley Hobson's
TOP 10 SUCCESS SQUARES

Be Fearless

Be Honest

Get Out of Your Comfort Zone

Create Attainable Goals

Take One Day at a Time

Give Yourself Some Love

Feed Your Body First

Pick the People you Want to Work With

Set a High Standard for Your Customers and Team

Go with the Flow

My evolution as a business owner would never have happened if I hadn't applied everything that I have learned. I credit not just the hard-edged lawyerly thinking I fine-tuned in college, but more the open-hearted spirit and love that yoga gives me.

These 10 Success Squares will guide you in building a successful business and team. I aim to be heart-centric in my approach with my clients and team members. Be authentic with your message, and run your business as a reflection of your values!

1. **Be fearless:** There is a reason you want to be doing something else in your life, right? Only by creating a new way to do things—listening to your highest voice for guidance, choosing to make positive change—can you create the future you know you deserve.

2. **Be honest:** If you are stuck in a job you're not jazzed up about anymore, a job that brings you DOWN instead of lifting you UP, then it is time to move on. It is essential that you look deeply into your heart, and find your "WorkTruth."

3. **Get out of your comfort zone:** When I left a career I thought was my destiny, I fell apart. No matter how tough you think you are, it is very easy to feel vulnerable, confused, fearful or even lost when faced with uncertainty. Change is constant. Adversity can be seen as a blessing. Instead of the F-you, give a big THANK you for being pushed towards your next "LifeStep." Real success comes when you spread your wings and fly!

Create Attainable Goals

4. **Create attainable goals, then push a little farther:** It's common to set yourself up with a truly unobtainable goal. This can be a way of staying frozen. Visualize success realistically… then keep pushing yourself as you learn more and enhance your skills.

Take One Day at a Time

5. **Take one day at a time:** I know it sounds like a cliché, but it's TRUE! Eat nourishing food. Exercise. Spend time with your friends. Do what has to be done TODAY— not tomorrow, not next week. I promise you that if you live one day at a time, you will secretly find yourself moving on.

Give Yourself Some Love

6. **Give yourself some love:** The relationship you have with yourself is the most important relationship you will ever have. If you can't take care of yourself with love and appreciation, you will never be able to take care of anyone else in your life. The better you feel about yourself, the more you will be able to attract the world around you.

Feed Your Body First

7. **Feed your body first:** Trust me on this one! I have been unhealthy at many points in my life, and my career suffered in those periods. Eating high vibration, fresh whole food will bring you the energy and focus you need to succeed.

8. **Pick the people you want to work with:** Nothing is more dangerous than working with the wrong team or group of people. If it feels difficult to choose one person or one group over another, trust in karma. All of our paths will unfold perfectly for all of us so there is no need to create any additional stress for yourself. When you are in alignment with yourself, you will attract the right people around you.

> **Pick the People You Want to Work With**

9. **Set a high standard for your customers and team:** Your clients are smarter than ever, and they require authenticity in both products and messaging. So do your team members. If you give your best to your universe, you will be paid back in spades. The New Consciousness requires an honest approach, high quality products, and a commitment to creating a better life for everyone.

> **Set a High Standard for Your Customers and Team**

10. **Go with the flow:** This is one of the most critical elements of my method. Without it, business—and life—may spin out of control...or so it may feel. In the flow, everything will be easier, and your business will be more successful if you live in the current moment and know that's the only moment you need to handle. Give it your full attention. It's your reality. And when that moment is over, move to the next moment. Are you ready for the next one that will bring you one step closer to engaging in your life again?

> **Go with the Flow**

Homemade Lavender Bath Salt

Ingredients

- 3 cups epsom salt
- 1 cup salt
- 2 cups baking soda
- 4 drops Lavender essential oil

Instructions

Mix together and enjoy!

Making your own bath salt is very simple, and chances are you already have all of these ingredients in your home. This makes a beautiful but inexpensive gift as well. Consider making a bunch for Mother's Day, for your child's teacher, or for your friend's birthday.

I absolutely love lavender but any essential oil works if you prefer a different scent.

Brown Sugar Honey Scrub

Ingredients

- 3 tbsp room temperature organic cold-pressed extra virgin olive oil
- 3 tbsp brown sugar
- 3 tbsp raw honey

Instructions

Mix together, rub in circular motions on face, then rinse and moisturize.

Feel free to add a few drops of your favorite essential oil to this scrub for aromatherapy benefits. Some of my favorites for a scrub are Orange and Geranium.

To purchase oils, please visit:
www.mydoterra.com/hayleyhobson

The anti-microbial properties and enzymes of raw honey, mixed with the exfoliating texture of sugar and the moisturizing fatty acids of olive oil make this a winning cleansing scrub for revealing radiant, glowing skin.

~ Chapter 7 ~
SEXUALITY

SHORT OR TALL. LARGE OR SLIM. BROWN, GREEN OR BLUE.

Auburn, brown or blonde. We are all so very different. And yet we beat ourselves up, comparing our height, our weight, the color of our eyes and our hair to everyone around us. How do you perceive yourself? Are you harsh and negative? Or do you manifest confidence? You are beautiful and sexy. Because the real beauty comes from simply being you. I realized a long time ago that I held the power to live a sexy and abundant life. Let me show you how.

Forty years old and my sex drive disappeared.

This is a super embarrassing story to tell, but unfortunately, it is the truth. When my daughter Madeline was born, my desire for sex and physical intimacy pretty much evaporated. Labor got kind of crazy just as I was pushing her out and it became clear I was going to either need a C-section or an episiotomy. I voted for the latter. Bummer for me—it was the equivalent of a third degree tear. I could barely walk for weeks after giving birth and was in pain long after my doctor told me I had "healed." Not to mention, I was sleep deprived and constantly exhausted. For all you mommas out there, I'm sure you're hearing me loud and clear.

For the first few weeks, when my husband was in the mood, I pulled the "baby card." But we can only get away with that for so long, right? Then the weeks slowly turned into months and the months even turned into years. I did not recognize the person I had become. My desire for sex had almost vanished. So what was I to do? Sexual connectivity and intimacy are supposed to nourish and strengthen the soul, and I had lost connection to that aspect of myself. As much as I wanted to talk to people about my problem, I was embarrassed and ashamed. The truth of the matter is, no one really talks about it, so I assumed everyone's sex life was perfect but mine.

I knew I needed help so I looked for guidance and support. First stop on my calendar was my OBGYN. I scheduled my annual appointment and guess what? He told me I was fine! Apparently I did not have any hormonal issues. I was totally in balance. Yeah right. So much for western medicine once again.

Next stop was my Ayurvedic doctor. His opinion was that I was totally out of whack, and until my life became more balanced, I most likely would not see any progress. Although the prognosis was not what I wanted to hear, it made sense to me. So what did I do? I changed my job. I changed my diet. I found a life coach. Wow. I didn't realize there was WAY more to my issues with sexuality than the minor surgical procedure I had not so long before.

I had lost my confidence. I had lost trust in both myself and in my husband. My insecurities were screaming at me. Most importantly, I was having trouble letting go. While I'm not here to give you an answer that is going to change your life, what I can tell you is if your sexuality is important to you, you must take a proactive stance in rediscovering yourself. You are going to have to begin to engage once again with a part of you that you've lost connection with —even if it's uncomfortable. As I'm sure you know, it's the uncomfortable road you take that gives you the freedom to grow.

What I've learned through my process is that losing connection to my sex drive is nothing to be ashamed of. It happens to more women than you would believe. I did not know it because most people are too ashamed or embarrassed to actually admit it! But at some point or another, many women, like me, disconnect from a part of themselves that used to be so seamless and effortless to connect to. Suddenly, that part of our lives requires work and effort.

As if we didn't already have enough on our plate! It seems easier to dodge the situation or withdraw in defense or shame. Honestly though, who does that really serve? Not you, and definitely not your partner. So don't you want to put that effort in? Of course you do. Both of you are so worth it.

I don't know about you, but I am always interested in pursuing passions that feed my soul. Those passions range from watching my toddler learn to swim or finish a 200-piece puzzle by herself, to getting deep within my own body in a yoga class, or spending a few cherished moments with my husband. What do they all have in common? Connection. Intimacy. It doesn't always have to be in the bedroom, but that's a great place to start—even when it feels like you have to carve out the time. I'm still learning to make it a priority, and believe me, it can be hard to find the time in this crazy busy world we live in.

Here are a few tips:

1. **Don't forget your inner goddess.** What makes you feel sexy, confident and ah-mazing? A warm bath? Skimpy underpants? A beautiful scent? If it dazzles you, it will dazzle your partner as well.

2. **Try alternative remedies** to help you improve your sex drive. For me it was supplementation in my diet, more live foods and pure, therapeutic essential oils. But you can also try acupuncture, Chinese herbs, Kundalini or Tantric Yoga. There are so many resources at your disposal to help you naturally reconnect to your sexuality.

3. **Slow down.** When life is a never-ending list of chores, sex can also start to feel like work. Life should be an exchange of dance and energy, not an obligation. Create space in your life for tenderness and healing. Invest in yourself and watch yourself transform.

It's always a process. Just let it unfold.

I felt ugly as a child. I was way too skinny.

My movements were awkward. My nose was too big. My hair was too curly. My jeans didn't fit right. I didn't even hit puberty until I was 16. I was the last kid picked to play on any team sport in gym class and the girl always without a boyfriend.

It wasn't until I went to college that my body started to fill out. My hair started growing. My face began to glow. My mother described my transformation as one from "ugly duckling" to "beautiful swan."

Yes, even my own mother was, let's say— relieved by my revolution.

All of a sudden, I was being noticed. I couldn't go anywhere without people looking at me. From the time I was 18 until I got married, I was never without a boyfriend. And when I broke up with one, it seemed as though there were plenty of men lining up to take the last one's place.

It was easy to go shopping. Everything fit. It was fun to go out at night. I was never lacking for someone with whom to have a conversation. I had loads of friends—both men and women.

I was no longer the skinny, ugly kid in class.

I felt beautiful. I felt sexy.

And because I FELT beautiful and sexy, my confidence soared. I went from being a child that would speak to no one, to a ring leader in my circle of friends. Party? I organized it. Dinner out? I sent out the invites. Location? I found it. The more the merrier. I was the hub of all activity.

But as I grew older and matured, I realized confidence doesn't have to have anything to do with beauty. And beauty has nothing to do with physical appearance.

I found what society would deem "gorgeous" women to be unappealing and instead found elegance and exquisiteness in non-traditional stereotypes. I fell in love with the idea of women owning their individuality and their power.

I re-found my sexiness in simply being ME.

They say that beauty is in the eye of the beholder. Ain't that the truth. And each and every single one of us has an inner beauty, an inner light, a divineness.

Each and every one of us is a goddess.

Remember that. Get out there and act like a diva. You are one.

10 Reasons to Have More Sex.

It's not a secret that sex sells or that just the mention of sex gets everyone a little hot under the collar.

Humans were designed to be sensual beings and are drawn to sex as a profound vehicle to connect, feel, experience pleasure and euphoria, make babies and love others.

When the time and space is 'right for sex,' sex can take you to other worlds. It can make you wonder why you are spending your time on anything but!

When it is on (and it is right) it can be the most potent and powerful experience in your life.

We all know sex feels good—but did you know there are incredible health benefits to sex as well?

So, the next time you diss your partner and tell him/her no...or the next time you find yourself wrapped up in your favorite television show (or whatever distracts you from not making sex an integral aspect of your life) and your partner wants to get it on, think about all the fun you are missing out on.

Sex is exercise; the more you have it, the better you will feel, the less likely you are to get divorced, break-up, find your man or woman cheating on you and the happier you may find yourself in your relationships.

Listen, people. Do whatever it takes if it's good for you. And if sex is where it's at start getting it on! No one likes a grumpus who'd rather text or check out on technology than get down.

Here are the health benefits of sex:

1. **Lower Blood Pressure:** The most basic health benefit of sex is lower blood pressure. Like any other form of cardio, an act that requires you to be 'active,' helps you stay calm in stressful situations, keeping your blood pressure down.

2. **Elevated Mental Outlook:** Lower stress levels also lead to a more elevated mental outlook. Sexually active people tend to be getting their needs met or actively playing a role in what the body needs, which decreases stress and leads to happier individuals.

3. **Boost Immunity:** As referenced in Web MD, sex has been shown to release chemicals that boost immunity, which means that having more sex could lead to better overall health and fewer colds. WOO HOO!

4. **Pain Relief:** During sex, chemical reactions can provide mild pain relief and even relieve migraine headaches according to according to Huffington Post for Women. I guess when you are blissed out or in that feel good euphoric state, pleasure kicks pain to the curb.

5. **Good for the Physique:** Sex is exercise. No matter what kind of sex you are having, whether it is energetic or you are spicing it up with sex toys, you are burning calories, releasing endorphins, working your muscles and sweating (at least I hope you are or you might be having some really bad sex.) Having a lot of sex won't win the war on weight or completely transform your body, but it helps and if you missed a run, go have some sex! At least you got some form of exercise in for the day.

6. **Better Self-esteem:** Sex boosts confidence, and makes you feel like a rockstar when it is on and it is great. There is nothing better than desiring another and having another desire you. It can plaster a permanent smile on your face—the one that screams I am on cloud nine.

7. **Spiritual Sense of Self-worth:** Some have claimed that sex can be a transcendental experience. It is a connection of energy or soul through the body, by which two people can explore non-ordinary highs. Some people claim that sex allows you to let go and experience yourself beyond ego and in this vein, make you feel connected to the universe or God, something bigger than ourselves. Everyone loves to experience highs rather than lows, and sex is a vehicle for this kind of connection.

8. **Intimacy Boost:** In romantic relating, sex boosts intimacy, which is the ability to connect beyond the act into a far deeper experience. We all want to experience the ability to completely abandon ourselves to an experience without losing ourselves. On some level, you can experience a deeper you through the other person. It is powerful when it is right.

9. **Healthy Heart:** An active sex life can keep the heart in good shape according to a article by Alternative Medicine. Just like regular exercise, an active sex life can give your heart the work out it needs, not just on an emotional level, but a physical level as well.

10. **Glowing:** Every sane person on this planet wants to put their best face forward and radiate light. The best way to get 'the glow' and exemplify this inner light is to get it on. Nothing sings a brighter song than a person who is sexually satisfied. You can be in the best shape of your life and have everything going for you in one vein, but if you are not getting your sexual needs met or sharing the kind of connection you need to thrive emotionally, you are missing the elixir of life. Getting your sexual needs met is vital to your health, on all levels.

I hope you enjoyed our little chat about all things sex. For those of you that feel a friend could use a dose of this yumminess, pass it along.

Chapter 7
YOGA SEQUENCE

1. BIDALASANA
2. ADHO MUKHA SVANASANA
3. PLANK
4. ADHO MUKHA SVANASANA
   (REPEAT 2-4, 3X)
5. RUNNERS LUNGE W/BLOCK
6. 1-LEGGED DOWNWARD DOG
7. CRESCENT LUNGE
8. SURYA NAMASKARA A
   (REPEAT 3X)
9. SPHINX
10. VIRABHADRASANA 2
11. TRIKONASANA
12. ARDHA CHANDRASANA
13. CHAPASANA
14. EKA PADA BHEKASANA
15. VINYASA
16. ONE LEGGED HIP OPENING SQUAT
17. EKA PADA RAJAKAPOTASANA
18. AGNISTAMBHASANA
19. BADDHA KONASANA
20. ARDHA MASTYANDRASANA
21. SIMPLE TWIST
22. SAVASANA

SURYA NAMASKARA A
(REPEAT 3X)

SEE PAGE 13

HIPS

 10

 14

 18

 22

 11

15

VINYASSA
SEE PAGE 13

 19

 12

 16

 20

 13

 17

 21

Visit **http://bit.ly/18w6vya** to access Hayley's downloadable Yoga class, *Core Yoga 4*.

Roasted Root Veggies with Tahini Sauce

Ingredients

- 5 cups root veggies, chopped uniformly (any combo of beets, turnips, rutabaga, fennel, carrots, parsnips or sweet potatoes)
- 1 red onion
- 2 tbsp coconut oil
- 1 big handful parsley, chopped

For the tahini dressing

- 1/2 cup tahini
- 1/2 cup cilantro
- 1 glove garlic, minced
- 1 tbsp Braggs Amino Acids
- Juice of 1 lemon
- 1/4 cup extra virgin olive oil
- 1 drop of Cilantro essential oil
- 3 drops of Lemon essential oil

Instructions

For the roots

Preheat the oven to 350 degrees. Add the essential oils to the liquified coconut oil, toss the veggies in it and then spread onto a baking sheet.

Bake for about 30 minutes or until slightly browned. Season with Himalayan Sea Salt and pepper; top with parsley. Serve as is or with tahini sauce.

For the dressing

Whisk or blend all ingredients together.

Raw Brownies

Ingredients

- 2 1/2 cups medjool dates (pitted, soaked in warm water for 5 mins)
- 2 cups raw walnuts
- 1/2 cup unsweetened cacao
- 1/2 cup unsweetened cacao nibs (optional, but highly recommended)
- 1 cup raw almonds (chopped, and soaked overnight)
- 2 tbsp chia seeds
- for sweeter brownies add 1 tbsp of agave nectar
- Pinch Himalayan Crystal Salt

Instructions

In a food processor, blend walnuts into a fine ground.

Add cacao powder and salt and pulse to combine then add dates individually until the mixture becomes 'crumby.'

In a square pan, press the walnut/cacao mixture down firmly pressing in the almonds, chia seeds and cacao nibs into the mixture.

Freeze for at least 2 hours and then slice into eighteen squares. Enjoy!

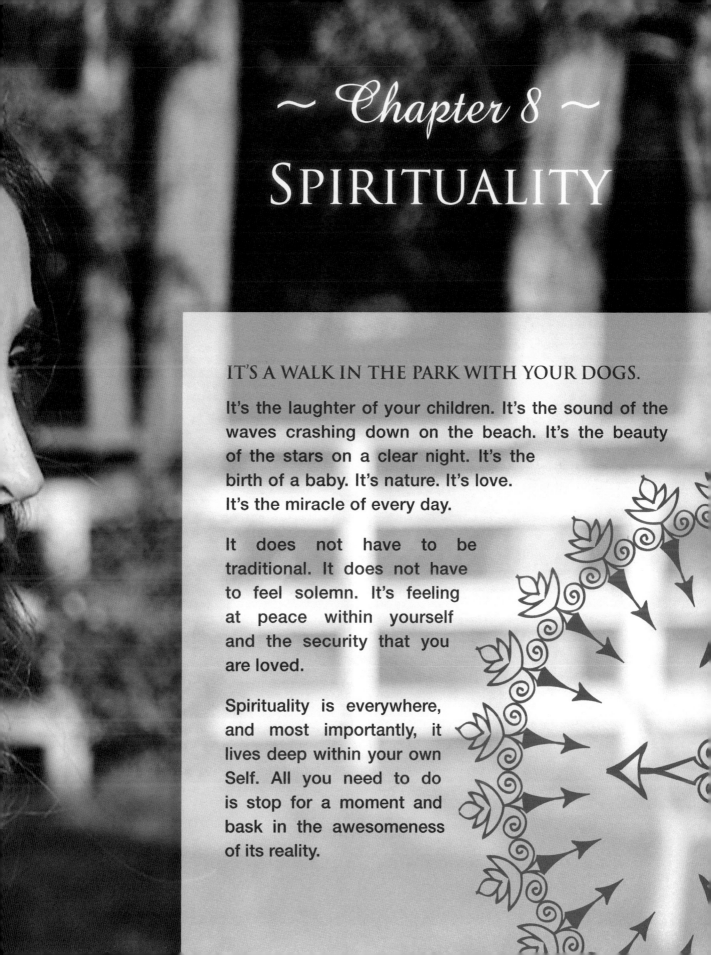

~ Chapter 8 ~
SPIRITUALITY

IT'S A WALK IN THE PARK WITH YOUR DOGS.

It's the laughter of your children. It's the sound of the waves crashing down on the beach. It's the beauty of the stars on a clear night. It's the birth of a baby. It's nature. It's love. It's the miracle of every day.

It does not have to be traditional. It does not have to feel solemn. It's feeling at peace within yourself and the security that you are loved.

Spirituality is everywhere, and most importantly, it lives deep within your own Self. All you need to do is stop for a moment and bask in the awesomeness of its reality.

What's your definition of "Power Yoga?"

I started practicing yoga in the mid 90's in Los Angeles. I can remember a line several blocks long around the Radio Shack at 6th and Santa Monica Blvd. I bet that line is still there when Bryan Kest is in town. His class was "by donation only" and he could pack at least 100 people in that room. He called it "Power Yoga." Although he worked us hard and by the end of each two-hour-plus class we were soaking wet, I can guarantee he did not intend his definition of Power Yoga to insinuate that his class was based in fitness.

A fitness routine, which is usually based on aesthetics, feeds your ego, not your soul. And when your ego is out of balance, you become more susceptible to the every day occurrences that are actually out of your control. A fitness routine focuses on how to get into a pose, not the actual results of each pose. But isn't the point of our yoga practice to strengthen our attentiveness and free ourselves of the distractions in our painfully cluttered minds?

Isn't the point to get us out of our competitiveness, our judgments? Out of our psyches?

When Bryan coined the term "Power Yoga," what I really think he intended to say is that *yoga is powerful.* He taught from his experience, which was to have the yoga create the highest level of vitality and freedom it can possibly have. It was to have the practice make you feel every sensation in your body and then allow you to move with that sensation.

When we work sensitively, we create an environment that's healing and that honors ourselves—an environment that respects our boundaries. We create an atmosphere that's conducive to natural expansion and growth. But in order to work sensitively, we need to take a seat and listen. This should make sense since the translation of asana means "seat." So, in each pose, we are supposed to sit and listen to the sensations. In each pose we allow time to bring circulation into our bodies, thereby regenerating our physical body and our spirit.

Once we listen and can actually feel what's going on in our bodies and are able to access places that need our attention and kindness, we are able to literally wake up. We can become enlightened. Hopefully. At least that's the ultimate goal—not to kick up into handstand in the middle of the room.

Why do we care if we can get up into a handstand anyway? Why do we care if we can even touch our toes? Who ever said a person who can go upside down or do Uttanasana with straight legs and a flat spine was more enlightened than the person who could not? If we are really that concerned what we look like in a pose, we must not like ourselves that much the way we were to begin with.

But how can we slow down to actually feel the intricacies in each pose when our teacher is shouting out, "inhale...lift your right leg high...exhale...step it through," faster than we can actually fully contract our diaphragm, because we're in a "power yoga" class? I don't know about you, but when I move that fast I feel like I'm a race-car driver racing around the track. I can't listen. I'm running a marathon! I'm out of alignment, imbalanced, suddenly negative and now I'm bringing into class all of the negative sh*t I meant to leave at the door.

Wasn't the "power" in my yoga supposed to be my humbleness and sense of calm? So that when I'm driving down US 36 and my 3-year-old tells me her "throw up is coming out," I can practice my "3-year-old-is-throwing-up-in-the-back-seat-of-my-car-asana?"

We've all stopped listening. The sad state of our planet is a prime example. Our egos and intellects have gotten so big, we've become enamored with ourselves and our capabilities. However, in order to listen to the innate wisdom within each and every one of us, we need to turn off our controlling minds. Then, by healing ourselves, we'll be able to help nurture our planet back to health.

The problem is, most people don't want to listen. And they surely don't want to do the work. So we start losing people to the calisthenics of yoga so they don't have to feel a friggin' thing.

I don't know about you but I'd like to practice yoga so that I can help facilitate a stillness inside and ultimately emancipate a deeper wisdom. Sounds powerful to me.

Which version of "power yoga" do you want to practice?

While growing up, I considered myself to be somewhat religious.

My family was Jewish so I went to synagogue, celebrated the Sabbath and had a bat-mitzvah. But all of this 'religious stuff' just felt like something I had to do, had to subscribe to—I didn't necessarily identify with it at a soul level. Religion was just like any other subject. It existed, I was taught that it was real, but I related to it in the same way I did the history on Henry the VIII.

I don't have memories of going to synagogue and feeling spirit or divinity move through me. I don't ever remember feeling touched by a GOD. What I do remember is having a lot of questions about the Torah, how people could really believe some of these stories were literal truths when science was constantly debunking these ideas: (ie, the story of Adam and Eve and the absence of dinosaurs in biblical history.)

Years later, I started practicing yoga. It took me a while, but after some time, while flowing through poses on my mat, feeling my breath move deeply in and out of body,

I began to I experience the feeling that something greater than myself existed. I finally felt what I think many people define as Spirit. It was energy. A force that moves through each and every one of us and connects all of us to each other. I had never known, before that moment, that such a force even existed or lived within me. I'm not sure what I even really thought about God. I had often questioned whether God was just an idea, an afterthought, or some kind of being I was supposed to believe in, but wasn't sure I even did. However, the more I practiced Yoga and continued to connect to my inner Self, the more familiar I became with God or Spirit or Mother Earth or whatever name you want to call it.

Spirit is a feeling, something ineffable, and yet completely experiential. Spirit feels like a presence—an experience of a deeper wisdom, inherent knowledge, awareness of something beyond what I see with my eyes. It is a feeling deep within my heart. I'm not really sure if everyone has the same experience with Spirit or what it means to be Spiritual. And I'm not sure that really matters. But I do know that when we pause for even a moment, we can feel something moving through us that we cannot explain. And I also know that experiencing the presence of this inexplicable force has truly altered my path.

Once you taste Spirit, you can never imagine your life without it. It's like a runner's high to be near it and feel the presence of such a force and energy you never thought was possible. When I am in the presence of Spirit, I feel loved. I feel cared for. I feel connected to all that is. I am able to tap into an inner guidance and wisdom that has not only allowed me to heal my own body, but has helped me to understand the needs of others as well.

For me it was my yoga mat. For you, it may be a walk in the moonlight on the beach. And to another, a thunderstorm. But for all of us, a common thread exists—living in accordance with nature with gratitude and compassion. Whatever it takes to allow breathe to move through your body, and help guide you and awaken your soul to come alive.

You don't have to be religious to be Spiritual. All you need is an awareness of Self and the ability to realize you are already connected to all living beings with no separation.

Barely into my twenties, I experienced my first heartbreak with a boyfriend I had thought I was meant to love for a lifetime.

I was young and naive. Full of ideals and fantasies. But we had different stories, different attachments and so, eventually, it had to end.

Little by little I began to realize our belief systems no longer aligned with each other. My life was moving forward, his was staying in place—in my opinion that is. So, no matter how in love we were, the relationship was not going to work.

I was heartbroken. I never thought I'd find the love of my life again.

And how could I feel SO strongly about someone who could not jump off the big cliff called life with me? Was this the cosmic joke? I had come so close to a love I believed was pure and real, only to discover it wasn't meant to last.

I moved to LA. He stayed back East. And we continued to torture each other over the phone. Until one day, just like that, it was over. Done.

I never saw him again.

There was no real ending. No peace. No grace to the finality. And I believe an ending like that did unspeakable damage to my soul.

Over night I went numb. Disconnected. Disassociated from reality. I couldn't cry. But I had no idea what was happening to me. I was young, and as I said, naive.

It was as if someone had shut the circuit breaker off inside of me and no one was home.

I'd walk into rooms of people never knowing where I was. I desperately wanted to connect but had no idea how.

I felt lost.

I went to therapists, healers, shamans —you name it. NO ONE could help me get to the root of my suffering or my disassociation.

I walked through my twenties and most of my thirties completely disconnected from my body. Men, women, relationships in general were superficial and didn't last. I knew deep down there was something wrong with me.

I couldn't feel. I couldn't taste. I couldn't love.

For years I lived with this condition I called disconnectedness.

Finally, I tried yoga. Not with the intention of connecting at first but miracles do happen. As I began to dig deeper, my shell started to soften. Like layers of an onion, my skin started to peel away.

And when my hardened exterior began to melt away, feelings finally rose to the surface. Emotions I didn't want to deal with. Sensitivities I didn't know I had. At first it was subtle. In fact, I may not even have noticed. As the days turned into months and the months turned into years, I began to see a shadow of myself lying next to me with light pouring out of my heart.

And you know what? There was no way I was going back in my box, soulless and alone.

Yoga, which had first sounded like the perfect new solution for maintaining a tight butt, helped reintegrate my spirit and connect me back to myself and back to my life.

I can now enjoy the taste of foods and the simple pleasures of life like my 3-year-old bossing me around or my husband and I cracking ourselves up over the same dumb-ass jokes.

I can finally see light.

Last Thursday, I woke up at 5:00 a.m. to hop an 8:00 a.m. flight to San Antonio.

I was picked up from the airport, proceeded to teach three classes that day at three different locations, drove to Austin the next morning to do the same thing, and then repeated my schedule in Houston on Saturday.

In-between classes and in the evening, I managed my online business, returned well over a hundred emails each day, managed to feed myself well, and even sneak in a run. Family was fine. I got a few calls in, even to my parents who complain when they haven't heard from me in forty-eight hours.

Saturday night on the plane back to Denver, I had some down time. As I was flying home, I couldn't stop thinking about the conversation I had had with one of my colleagues. She still hadn't followed up with a few leads we had received a few weeks before because she couldn't find the time.

You know what I hate more than anything? The excuse that someone does not have enough time in her day. C'mon people! We ALL have the same twenty-four hours in one day. No one has any more. No one has any less. So the issue is not that you don't have the time; the issue is how you choose to use it.

Every single person on this planet is given the gift of life, but the vast majority don't know how to show up. I hear it all the time: I coulda, woulda, shoulda.

Don't be that person living for the future, stuck in the past, or fantasizing about the person you want to be, think you are, or will become tomorrow. If you want to get it done, DO IT.

The only thing that exists is the moment *right here, right now.* I know you want to stop making excuses. I know that sometimes it feels like you can't get over that hurdle of whatever holds you back. I know that believing in yourself would be easier if someone else pushed you, challenged you, or believed in you. But guess what? This isn't about anyone else but YOU and what YOU are going to do with the time you are given.

It's really simple. You have two choices: You either bitch and whine and pretend to be something you want to be but aren't, or you find a way to get beyond your excuses and capture the life you seek.

Please don't be one of those people who always finds an excuse.

Be one of those people who makes magic happen.

Don't live vicariously through reality TV stars and celebrity lore.

Visual *your* life the way *you* want it. Not just once, but multiple times. The power of visualization will then control your actions.

You can either die with a fist full of regrets or you can rest in peace knowing you actually applied yourself by discovering what you are made of.

Don't you hate it when you hear people telling their friends (or strangers) what to do and how to live their lives?

Geez! I even find myself doing that every once in a while. Or, you may read a blog online that says, "Just open your heart" as if it's a no-brainer. But what if it's difficult? What happens when coming from the heart makes you feel like you're stuck behind a thick pane of glass and there's a disconnect between where you stand and the world out there?

Can you snap your fingers, just like that, and open your heart?

If you can, you're blessed.

I couldn't always open my heart with the snap of a finger. There have been times in my life when I couldn't wrap my mind around what it meant to do so.

In retrospect, I now realize I couldn't wrap my mind around it because in order to do so, I'd have to *feel.*

We have to experience. No measure of logic will help. When the heart opens, so does the mind.

If you're anything like me, and you struggle with coming from a place of heart, here are some easy exercises that will help you open and heal.

While they may seem difficult at first, just practice. Eventually they'll become second nature.

1. Find a quiet place to sit down.
2. Close your eyes and breathe in through your nose, deep down to your belly, making sure to allow your breath to touch your heart on the way down.
3. As you sit there, allow in all of the memories or moments you've had in your life that have touched your heart.
4. Allow what you love or what moves your heart to come to the surface.

Many of us shove our true feelings and experiences out of our hearts at a very young age as a result of trauma or neglect. Most of us don't even realize we are that disconnected until a major blowout transpires around us, showing us just how much pain we're really in. Staying inside of our hearts is vital to our emotional well being.

Any measure of "real time" you give yourself will help you stay connected to your heart and feelings.

So take a breath, let go, open your heart and get connected to yourself.

Chapter 8
YOGA SEQUENCE

1. BIDALASANA
2. ADHO MUKHA SVANASANA
3. ANAHATASANA
4. ADHO MUKHA SVANASANA
   (REPEAT 1, 2, 3 - 2X)
5. SURYA NAMASKARA A
   (REPEAT 3X)
6. GOAL POST ARMS
7. VRKASANA
8. CRESCENT LUNGE W/ARMS
   CLASPED BEHIND BACK
9. PARSVAKONASANA WITH WRAP
10. TRIKONASANA
11. ARDHA CHANDRASANA
12. VINYASA
13. VASISTASANA VARIATIONS
14. WILD THING
15. SETU BANDHA SARVANGASANA
16. URDHA DANURASANA
17. SUPTA HASTA PADANGHUSTASANA
18. HAPPY BABY
19. SIMPLE TWIST
20. SAVASANA

SURYA
NAMASKARA A

(REPEAT 3X)
SEE PAGE 13

WILD THING

VINYASA -
SEE PAGE 13

Visit **http://bit.ly/TxARZ5**
to access Hayley's downloadable
Yoga class, *Empowerment Flow*.

Avocado Bliss Soup

Ingredients

- 2 avocados
- 1 medium cucumber
- 2 stalks celery
- Juice of 1 small lime
- Handful of fresh cilantro
- 2 tsp cumin
- 1 tsp ground coriander
- 1/2 tsp Himalayan Sea Salt
- 1 tsp Braggs Amino Acids
- 1 cup water
- Chives and pumpkin seeds to garnish
- 1 drop Cilantro essential oil
- 1 drop Lime essential oil

Instructions

Blend all ingredients, except the essential oils and the chopped chives in a high-speed blender until smooth. Once blended, add essential oils and stir gently. Then add chives and seeds to garnish.

Raw Onion Crackers

Ingredients

- 2 white onions
- 2 carrots
- 2 celery stalks
- 1/2 cup olive oil
- 1/2 cup walnuts
- 1/2 cup sunflower seeds
- 1/4 cup chia seeds
- 1/4 cup flax seeds

Instructions

Add all ingredients to a high speed blender. Take mixture from blender and lay out out flat on dehydrator sheet. Dehydrate at 110 degrees overnight (or longer if you like them crunchier.)

And Finally...

~ Chapter 9 ~

BRINGING IT ALL TOGETHER

IT MAY SEEM DIFFICULT TO MANAGE ALL THAT LIFE PRESENTS TO YOU ON A DAILY BASIS.

If you're working as hard as it takes to survive these days, you may ask yourself, "How does anyone find time to prepare a meal, let alone a nutritious one?"

If you are raising children, you and your partner may get frustrated that you can't even find a few moments a day to create the romance that once brought you together.

You may feel as though you're taking care of everyone else but yourself and you know you need to slip away more often than you've been allowing yourself—so that you can rejuvenate and come back with energy and vitality.

I have been there. I empathize. That's why I'm sharing my tips called "Hayley Hobson's Healthy Habits" with you. They are about establishing boundaries, guidelines or rules that will allow you to live, grow, and evolve into the finest version of yourself you can.

Are you ready to move in the right direction?

Hayley Hobson's **Healthy Habits**

1. You don't need to be Superwoman. Let go of perfection and watch yourself soar.

2. Feed your body the real food and love it needs to survive. Plants are nature's medicine. Eat more of them.

3. Get out there and move! Do something you enjoy to get your juices flowing.

4. Open your heart with compassion, love and gratitude with no expectations.

5. Treat yourself as good as, if not better, than you are treating others around you. Conserve your energy so that you can teach your children, and make effective changes around you.

6. Love what you do for a living. You have the ability to author your life in any direction you choose. You have every right to turn your passions into your career.

7. Be the goddess that you are. Don't be afraid to shine your light on everyone around you.

8. Pause. Breathe. Soak it in. Give gratitude for the big picture.

9. It's a walk in the park with your dogs. It's the laughter of your children. It's the sound of the waves crashing down on the beach. It's the beauty of the stars on a clear night. It's the birth of a baby. It's nature. It's love. It's the miracle of every day.

10. It does not have to be traditional. It does not have to feel solemn. It's feeling at peace within yourself and the security that you are loved.

11. Spirituality is everywhere and most importantly it lives deep within your own self. All you need to do is stop for a moment and bask in the awesomeness of its reality.

7-Day Vegan Detox Program

A Detox program you will not be afraid to try. I'm talking all real food. No gimmicks. It's not intimidating. There is no fasting. It's for real and it's easy. Why a Vegan Detox? It's cleaner. It does the job. You don't have to be afraid. And...it's only 7 Days.

To purchase program, please visit:
www.hayleyhobson.com/7-day-detox-program

The Last 5 lbs. – 14 Day Reset Program

It's easy. It's doable. It's adaptable. It works. And guess, what – you can do it from anywhere. You're on top of your game. You just need a refresher. You've been there before but need to brush up. The Last 5 lbs. program is for YOU if you're looking to fine tune your diet, the foods you nourishing your body with and your attitude.

Are you ready to take the next step towards loving your body and loving your life? Are you ready to become that healthy, svelte, awesome version of yourself? The Last 5 lbs. in 14 Days Nutrition Program is designed for you to feel slim and fabulous.

To purchase program, please visit:
www.hayleyhobson.com/last-5-lbs

30-Day Flab to Fab Nutrition Program

You know you want it but something keeps holding you back. You're going to a party. Your family is coming to town. You've got a trip planned. You've never been successful before at dieting. You think you know exactly what to eat. Believe me, I've heard it all. GUESS WHAT – My program is not intimidating. It's doable. Feasible. With loads of information you probably didn't know you needed to make your body look and feel its best. AND you can do it anytime and from anywhere. And trust me, you'll go from Flab to FAB in just 30 days. There is no excuse.

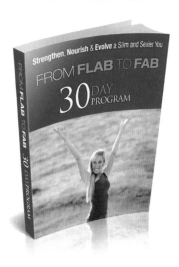

My 30-Day From Flab To Fab Program is designed for you to feel slim and fabulous. How does it work? I teach you Nutrition 101 and how to eat! It's that easy. Your body will respond. And when you treat it well, it will give back to you in the form of energy and a more positive outlook.

Isn't it time to feel alive again?

To purchase program, please visit:
www.hayleyhobson.com/30-day-nutrition-program

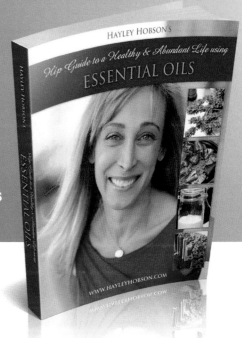

Hayley's Hip Guide to a Healthy & Abundant Life Using Essential Oils

To purchase ebook, please visit:
www.hayleyhobson.com/hayleys-books

Marie Forleo's B-School

Make Money. Change The World. Become your own entrepreneur.
There really is no other way.
www.rhhbschool.com

Institute for Integrative Nutriton

Holistic Nutrition that will Transform your Body, Mind & Soul. A mind-blowing
experience and the best choice you'll ever make.
www.integrativenutrition.com

BodyMind Institute

The ONLY Raw Nutrition Certification.
www.bodymindinstitute.com/affiliate/scripts/click.php?a_aid=hayleyhobson

Pangea Organics Skincare

Experience Beauty Unpolluted with organic, gluten-free, vegan, non-GMO skin care. Don't you want to put the very best on your skin? I know I do.

www.pangeaorganics.com/hayleyhobson

doTERRA Certified Pure Essential Oils

Experience Holistic Medicine. Become your own Pharmacist. Natural. Safe. Pure. Effective. Guaranteed. I wouldn't want it any other way.

www.mydoterra.com/hayleyhobson

ABOUT THE AUTHOR

HAYLEY HOBSON

Hayley Hobson is an author, speaker, business coach, yogi, Pilates and holistic nutritional expert based in Boulder, CO. Hayley creates lifestyle transformations by coaching her clients to strengthen, nourish and evolve through the cycles and shifts in life. Combining cutting edge understanding in all three disciplines due to years of anatomical study and dietary theory, Hayley's approach leverages their blended benefits and results. Her unique and intelligent style promotes strengthening while softening– empowering her client's to heal not only their physical bodies, but their hearts and minds as well. Hayley studied at the Institute for Integrative Nutrition, continues her studies with David Wolfe, raw food expert, and is an essential oil expert in her own right.

Hayley is a doTERRA Certified Pure Essential Oil Diamond Director and a Pangea Beauty Ecologist. Her insights and articles can also be found on her **blog, *Positively Positive, Mindbodygreen, Elephant Journal, Mastershift* and *Natural Cures.*** She has also been featured in ***Pilates Style magazine, Natural Health magazine*** and ***Triathlete Magazine.*** She has fun running and playing in the mountains with her husband, former world-ranked triathlete, Wes Hobson and their two beautiful daughters, Makenna and Madeline.

To learn more about Hayley's nutritional courses, events she's hosting, and custom programs, visit **www.hayleyhobson.com** and follow her on **Facebook**, **Twitter** and **Pinterest**.

Made in the USA
San Bernardino, CA
21 June 2014